The Stream Garden

ARCHIE SKINNER AND DAVID ARSCOTT

WARD LOCK

A WARD LOCK BOOK

First published in the UK in 1994
by Ward Lock
Villiers House
41/47 Strand
London WC2N 5JE

A Cassell Imprint

Distributed in the United States by
Sterling Publishing Co., Inc.
387 Park Avenue South, New York, NY 10016-8810

Distributed in Australia by
Capricorn Link (Australia) Pty Ltd
2/13 Carrington Road, Castle Hill, NSW 2154

British Library Cataloguing-in-Publication Data
A catalogue record for this book is available from the British Library

ISBN 0-7063-7154-2

Typeset by Method Limited, Epping, Essex

Printed and bound in Spain by Cronion S.A., Barcelona

Contents

Acknowledgements

Our thanks to the landscape and garden design consultant Nigel Philips, creator of the suburban case study garden, for agreeing to our close involvement in all stages of the project.

The publishers would like to thank Stapeley Water Gardens for donating material used in the construction of the suburban stream garden in Chapter 4.

Photographs supplied by Heather Angel (p. 50); Pat Brindley (p. 85); Stuart Cooper (p. 75); EWA (p. 109); Jerry Harpur (pp. 6, 24, 28, 107); Andrew Lawson (p. 40); Clive Nichols (pp. 58, 97, 100, 119); Hugh Palmer (pp. 47, 53, 57, 91); Archie Skinner (pp. 67, 71, 72, 73, 74, 76, 77, 78, 79, 117); Harry Smith Horticultural Photographic Collection (p. 27); Wildlife Matters (pp. 21, 81, 87, 92).

Line illustrations by Nils Solberg.

Introduction

We begin with a mystery: why is it that so few of us dare to introduce into our gardens that most magical of natural effects, the living, dancing presence of running water? Who, after all, can resist it? The sounds and shimmering of running water, gurgling through narrow channels and splashing over rocks, have an obvious fascination for young and old alike.

It is, moreover, an immensely varied pleasure. A water feature responds, like the living thing it is, to the changing seasons and the vagaries of the weather. What is usually a trickle may become a torrent after heavy rain, the water dashing over cascades when once it only spattered. The reflective surface of a pool at the stream's end will tremble in a vigorous breeze, making ever-changing patterns of light and shade, but in deep winter its ripples may be transformed into a thick coating of ice.

We suspect that a gross exaggeration of the difficulties involved has been the chief deterrent to creating streams. The least scientific among us knows that water flows downhill, and the owner of a flat plot is likely to feel that tampering with the contours will require labour sufficient to rebuild the Pyramids of Egypt. The owner of a dry garden may believe that the introduction and circulation of water will be vastly expensive.

Opposite: Meandering and rock-strewn this stream artfully disguises its artificial origins.

This is not so. Any gardener who already has a pond needs little equipment to enliven an otherwise static plot with a busy, chattering stream, and although careful planning will obviously be necessary, the gardener who has no water at all can introduce it without very much difficulty.

It would be foolish to deny that a certain amount of heavy work is inevitable or to pretend that a pump and other equipment cost no money, but amateur gardeners of modest means happily erect greenhouses and sturdy sheds, build patios and terraces and fashion flowerbeds and vegetable patches from the most unpromising wasteland. In the context of that degree of devoted and unstinting attention, the stream garden is by no means an unattainable luxury.

Almost any garden can benefit from the introduction of water, since every feature may, with sensitivity, be scaled down to suit its environment, but some gardens positively cry out for it. An unregarded wet and boggy area, for instance, may be drained into a pool or a series of pools through the construction of an artfully designed stream bed, thereby almost magically realizing its hidden potential – suddenly this part of the garden has a reason for existing. Many a dry, difficult, flat and uninspiring site will be utterly transformed when the soil that has been dug out for the new pond and stream is used to create natural-looking slopes and contours, and those fortunate gardeners who are already blessed with natural streams can enhance them by judicious planting and the introduction of dams, bridges and stepping-stones.

The range of wildlife attracted to the garden will be significantly increased. Fish, frogs, toads and newts will live in the pool; mayflies and dragonflies will hover above it; wagtails and other birds will skim over its surface.

As for the plants that can be grown there, the variety of habitats that will be created in even a small space will allow an impressive range to be introduced. There will be those, such as water lilies (*Nymphaea* species) and the water hawthorn (*Aponogeton distachyos*) with its scented white flowers, that will thrive in the middle of the pool. Others – the pretty white bog bean (*Menyanthes trifoliata*), the blue-flowered pickerel weed (*Pontederia cordata*), moisture-loving irises and the flowering rush (*Butomus umbellatus*) with its tall heads of pink flowers, for example – will enjoy the muddy conditions at the pool edges and the shallows of the stream. The stream banks can be made colourful with hostas, Siberian flag (*Iris sibirica*), astilbes and ferns, all of which enjoy moist areas but will not thrive when their roots are permanently water-logged.

Almost without exception, the plants used in the stream garden are hardy. In addition, most of these plants may be propagated by division, which means that the patient gardener can eventually stock a large area at little cost. Moreover, many of them, such as hostas, are excellent ground-cover plants, which will minimize the necessary labour of weeding.

The whole emphasis of this book is on the natural look. We shall, of course, use artifice but only to ensure that the complete scheme gives the impression of having evolved over a considerable period of time. The hard edges will be softened by plants, and the shape of the pool or stream will seem to have been carved by nature. There will be no straight lines, but only the gentle curves that, for us, represent true beauty of expression.

Because our own preference is for the natural-looking water garden, we concentrate on the techniques that will produce that effect. You will, therefore, find in these pages no crazy-paving or fake stone; no fountains or wishing-wells with their attendant gnomes; no atmospheric underwater lighting to illuminate quaint grottoes. These features may have their place, but it is not here.

You will probably wish to incorporate one or more ponds in your stream garden – and, for us, a pond is a pool, a basin of water that appears to have accumulated its plants and wildlife without human agency. The typical stream will run from a header pool at its highest level to a lower pool, which contains a submersible pump to keep the water circulating around the system. Numerous variations on the theme are possible. If the garden is big enough, you might introduce a number of pools along the course of a winding stream, with dams to create tinkling cascades. Where space is strictly limited, however, there might be no header pool at all – the stream can simply be fed from a concealed pipe.

Indeed, the techniques outlined here are infinitely adaptable. The introduction of a pool will not suit every taste or every lifestyle. Parents of young children, for example, may regard the lure of still water as too dangerous. One possible solution is to feed a shallow stream from an enclosed and buried tank. Similarly, your 'stream' may be nothing more than a trickle of water along a rocky bed until such time as safety is no longer an issue and the flow can be increased. There is no rule that cannot be broken to effect.

The practical advice contained in this book should enable you to undertake the necessary design, construction work and maintenance for a successful stream garden.

1

Designing the Stream Garden

Running water unifies a garden. All the different elements within a garden relate to the stream, and, as you will discover, all your visitors will make a bee-line for it. Beware, therefore; for as with any other prominent garden feature, it is essential that great care is taken over the initial design.

If you already have running water in your garden you are supremely fortunate. You will, of course, be dependent on rainfall to some extent, but you may be able, with only the minimum of work, to enhance its natural appearance and increase the range of wildlife it attracts. You can make the existing stream more of a feature simply by contouring and planting the approaches to it. You may, on the other hand, feel that the watercourse is too close to an eyesore or too far from your house and wish to divert its course within your own property, which will inevitably involve you in some hard labour.

Gardeners who already have a pond may well be able to make it a part of their new feature, although it would be unwise to design the stream to take an otherwise unsatisfactory route simply to accommodate an existing pool. It might be better to fill in the existing pond and start again than to regret an ugly design later.

Whatever your ambitions, take a serious look at the whole area and approach any re-landscaping or diversion as if it were a completely new feature.

Whether you are redesigning an existing stream or creating your stream garden from scratch, it is worth taking time to consider exactly what you want and what would best suit your needs and the style of your garden.

THE BASIC DESIGN

The route of the stream must be considered before all else. You must decide how it will best adapt to its surroundings and link the various existing elements of your garden. Your initial plans will almost certainly be amended as you play around with the possibilities, but the stream itself should be your top priority.

Once you have decided on the course and dimensions of the stream it will be time to consider the many possible features that will enhance its appeal. Pools are an obvious choice, and, unless you decide against them for reasons of safety, we would recommend that you have one at the lowest point of your garden into which the running water will fall. In addition to the obvious attraction of a pool, it is a good place to position an electric pump.

The more ambitious your water feature, the more likely you are to want more than one pool along the route of the watercourse, but even if you decide against this because of the constraints of space, it is worth considering siting a second pool immediately above the first. This will give you the delightful sound of falling water in a small area – an effect you could achieve by installing a fountain although at the expense of a natural look.

The aim of achieving a natural effect should also apply to the use of dams, bridges, stepping-stones and seats, which are discussed later in this chapter.

DRAWING A PLAN

Whatever features and elements you consider including, it is important not to rush into any decisions, particularly if the garden itself is new to you. You will probably find it helpful to buy some graph paper and mark the dimensions of your house and garden on it. Once you have chosen a preferred route for your stream, draw straight lines on the paper showing the angle of vision from various vantage points in and around the house. There is no point in designing features that can hardly ever be seen.

What works on paper, however, will not necessarily work in practice. The initial planning is vital so that you can give order to your ideas, but only by knowing your garden thoroughly can you hope to make the right decisions. Begin to refine your initial plan. Use stakes, rope or a long hose-pipe to mark out the principal features – pool, stream, sitting areas and so on – and watch where the sunlight falls at different times of the day and at different times of the year, so that you can avoid introducing plants to shady areas where they cannot

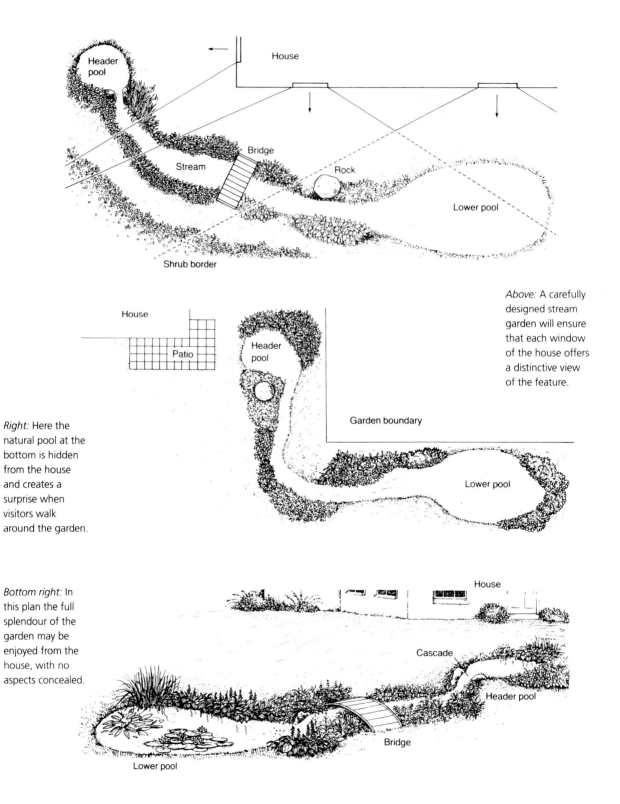

Above: A carefully designed stream garden will ensure that each window of the house offers a distinctive view of the feature.

Right: Here the natural pool at the bottom is hidden from the house and creates a surprise when visitors walk around the garden.

Bottom right: In this plan the full splendour of the garden may be enjoyed from the house, with no aspects concealed.

This design makes the most of a narrow rectangular garden. The planting near the bridge conceals the upper pool and summer house

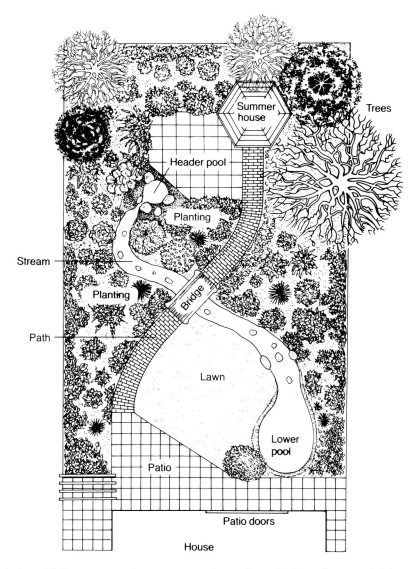

Trees

Summer house

Header pool

Planting

Stream

Planting

Bridge

Path

Lawn

Lower pool

Patio

Patio doors

House

thrive. Make a note of any areas where the wind tends to swirl (as uncomfortable for people as for plants), and notice the drier and damper parts of the garden. There is no substitute for this kind of first-hand knowledge.

As a general rule, the water feature should take up to no more than one-third of the whole garden. Scale is all-important, and an entire landscape of large pools and tinkling rivulets is likely to feel unnatural. The water should not be so dominant that it distracts your attention from other attractive features or views. A small stream, suddenly discovered on a walk around the garden, may well fit into the overall scheme of things better than a swirling torrent.

POSITIONING THE POOL

Other things being equal, it is best to place your pool in an open area, away from the heavy shade of trees you wish to retain. This is an important consideration because strong light promotes sturdy growth, and plants such as water lilies and water hawthorn love full sunshine – ideally, 5–6 hours free of shade every day. In addition, fallen leaves decompose in the water and form toxic gases that are harmful to fish and other water life. If this kind of site cannot be avoided be prepared for frequent cleaning of the pool.

Another consideration when you are thinking about the position of the pool is the availability of water to fill it and electricity to power the pump. You can dig a channel to carry the cable in a pipe, but do bear in mind the inconvenience of tunnelling long distances or of excavating for the wiring at some time in the future should there be a problem with it. Because a buried or camouflaged flexible pipe will be needed to carry the pumped water from the pool to the head of the stream, you should also calculate the logistics of excavating and constructing this right at the outset (see Chapter 2).

DESIGNING THE POOL

Your drawn plans should include the shape of your pool, and many gardeners have developed an excellent eye for how things will look when they are completed. Nevertheless, there is nothing like seeing the actual outline on the ground, and you will find it very helpful to mark it out with a length of rope or, if it is sufficiently flexible, your hose-pipe. If possible, leave the marker down for a few days, moving it around until you are completely satisfied with the shape. View the garden from all possible angles, including upstairs rooms if you live in a house with more than one storey.

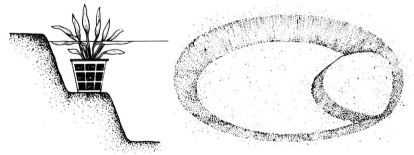

Shelving in the pool will allow you to introduce a variety of species.

runs through rich vegetation. If you choose this style, parts of the water's surface will be hidden from view, so presenting you with unexpected glimpses of water as you walk around the garden. The need for more maintenance will be offset by the advantages of additional colour and textures and the greater numbers of birds and wild animals that will be attracted to the stream.

JAPANESE WATER GARDENS

The Japanese were among the first to introduce water into gardens, and over the centuries they refined and perfected the imitation of the natural landscape in the domestic setting, this recreation of nature acting as an object for contemplation and a subject for philosophy. The creation of a true Japanese garden is beyond the scope of this book, and it would, in any case, require several years' study. Some of the Japanese ideas for using water may, however, be usefully applied in gardens that are otherwise thoroughly western in concept.

'Hill and pond' is one of the five basic styles used in Japanese gardening, the artificial landscape echoing the grander scale of mountains and oceans in the natural world. Not only is scale important in such a garden, but rocks are chosen with the utmost care and trees are artfully pruned for a windswept effect. Water may be used in the smallest areas, and if space is at a premium in your own garden, you may want to consider the techniques of *tsukubai* (running water basin) and *shishi-odoshi* (deer-scarer), each of which requires the use of a small pump.

A dry creek, rather than running water, is an option that requires little maintenance; the stream bed is scattered with small stones and gravel. This approach is suitable for gardeners with young children, worried about the dangers of having a pool. Running water can easily be introduced at a later stage.

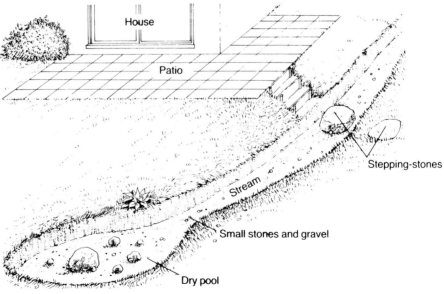

House

Patio

Stepping-stones

Stream

Small stones and gravel

Dry pool

Japanese gardens make skilful use of stone. Here the boulders in the foreground complement the round clumps of shrub.

In *tsukubai* a bamboo pipe drips water into a basin, which may be nothing more than a large, hollowed-out stone. Traditionally these were placed on the verandah with a wooden ladle beside them so that refreshment was always to hand. Hygiene probably suggests otherwise today. However, this style is certainly very suitable for bringing moving water to a limited area close to a house, possibly on a patio.

The *shishi-odoshi* technique involves pivoting a bamboo stem, the 'scarer', unevenly on a fulcrum and driving its motion with gently flowing water. The shorter end of the stem catches drops of water, tilting it to the ground. As the water is released, so the longer, heavier end falls to the ground, striking the underlying stone and resonating. Water fills the shorter end, and the process is repeated.

There was, for a period, a fashion in Japan for representing lakes and rivers by means of dry creeks strewn with sand, pebbles and boulders, and this practice is followed to this day where no water is available. This technique would be suitable for gardens where no more than a trickle of water is desired.

ALTERNATIVE STREAM DESIGNS

For every problem there is a solution, and many of the best gardeners have used running water in ways that can be usefully copied or adapted for your own plot.

A simple and extremely effective variation for shallow running water is a technique sometimes used the by British garden designer Gertrude Jekyll (1843–1932), who often worked in association with the architect Sir Edwin Lutyens (1869–1944). Here a narrow rill descends by the gentlest of gradients over a bed of slates. These slates are placed on edge, close together in the cement bottom of the watercourse to give a rippling, glittering effect.

Opposite: Boulders of different sizes give the impression of having been washed downstream by flooding. The hosta leaves echo the shape of the rocks beneath, while contrasting with the overhanging Japanese maple.

If your stream has lengths of continuous flat stone, with water running over a shallow bed, you might want to consider leaving occasional gaps between the rocks so that the water fills small basins within the stream. Such miniature pools will add interest to a design and, at times when the pump is switched off, will reflect light and give life to an otherwise static scene.

Too many ingenious devices in your water feature will, however, make it look like a self-conscious designer's showpiece. They are fine in their place, but will not give the natural effect for which we are striving. It might be more appropriate to set different sized rocks and boulders along the bed of the watercourse to interrupt the flow and produce light-reflecting ripples. Use rocks that are the same material as your dam so that they will appear to have broken away from it and have been carried downstream.

Slates packed on edge provide a bed over which shallow water will glitter and glisten.

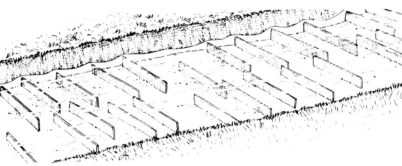

ADDITIONAL GARDEN FEATURES

Remember that your stream must be integrated into your garden in as natural a way as possible, and your initial design and construction plans must take account of the whole landscape.

CROSSING THE STREAM

If your stream is wide enough to require a means of crossing you might want to consider stepping-stones. These must straggle rather than march in a straight line – aim for a studied irregularity – and they must blend in with their surroundings. Select rocks that are flat and heavy so that their weight makes them firm to step on, and place higher rocks on the bank at either side to provide a hand-hold for the

unsteady. If you are laying the rocks on a liner, protect the liner by making sure that they are seated firmly in beds of waterproof cement.

If you opt for a bridge you could use a fallen tree, although you must think about who will be using it, for some of your visitors may not be agile enough to clamber over a moist and slippery beech trunk. Consider covering the wood with wire-netting to prevent people slipping, and a rustic handrail would be a help, too. A sturdier bridge could be made from two lengths of oak, with the ends shaved off to stop them rolling, and about 90cm (3ft) apart. Slats of treated chestnut, about 2.5cm (1in) thick and 7.5cm (3in) wide, could be nailed to the trunks and covered with wire-netting to provide a non-slip surface.

Bridges of stone or planks will obviously be artificial, but they should fit into the landscape if you keep to a simple design. Moving water reflected on stone can create magical effects.

Below: While stones of this size and shape may be difficult to acquire, and certainly to handle, they give solidity and a feeling of permanence. The stone on the right has been raised to allow water to flow under it.

Opposite: Rigid horizontal lines at eye level should be avoided wherever possible, but if a bridge demands a handrail, as here, a simple, rustic design is best.

DAMS

Dams are a means of holding back the water and slowing its flow, thereby making pools of still water that will create reflections. They will also produce the sound of water in a variety of ways, depending on their construction and the amount of water flowing over them. A further effect of a dam is to accentuate the different levels of the design, as was achieved in the suburban garden described in Chapter 4.

For the sake of economy and efficiency a dam may be made of concrete, but it must be faced with rock if you want to achieve a natural

Chiselling narrow grooves in the flat surface of a dam will cause the water to ripple and glitter as it flows over. A splash rock at the bottom prevents gouging out of the base.

Creating narrow gaps in the stonework at the top of the dam will increase both the movement and the sound of the water. Again, a splash rock should be placed below.

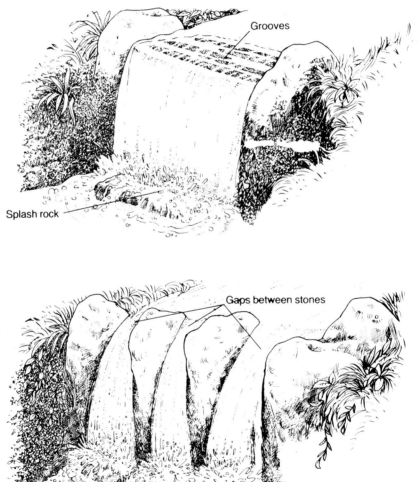

26

effect, and, as in all rock gardening, it is important to mimic the natural strata. The dams must look as if they are outcrops – vertical rocks suggest disturbance and introduce an unwelcome element of chaos.

If there is no alternative to unadorned concrete, make sure that you roughen the surface to give it as natural an appearance as possible and to encourage the colonization of lichen, which will quickly become established if the air is sufficiently clean.

The finish that you give the top of the dam is important because this will influence the flow of the water over the cascade and affect the sound it makes. Water will spurt through a small, narrow channel but glide over a broad, flat surface, and if you chisel narrow grooves in the rock you will induce a glittering effect. A rock placed a little way downstream – as if it had been dislodged from the dam and borne away by the current – will produce more movement as the water flows over and around it.

The projecting lip of the dam creates a cascade of water that froths and bubbles in the stream beneath. The water-tugged leaves of the rush emphasize the strength of the flow of water.

PATHS

Above: Steps made of wood, logs or stone are less obtrusive. Here planting covers the edges of the stone, and from the far side of the stream the steps are camouflaged by flag iris, ferns and meadow sweet.

Access to the water is obviously crucial, but the last thing you want in a natural landscape is a path that looks like a public right of way. It may be sufficient to cut the grass shorter along the preferred route than elsewhere, but, whatever you do, the course must be varied so that at times it is close to the water and at other times further away, through the plantings, so that the view changes constantly.

You may choose to make your path of dark-coloured gravel, wood chips or roundels of wood – oak or beech with a non-slip surface of wire-mesh are best. Whatever material you choose, however, it should not distract the eye from the water or the plants.

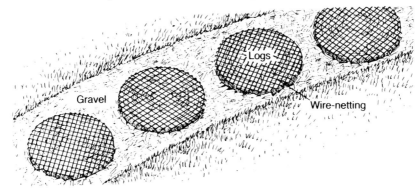

Left: Logs set up in gravel make a natural-looking path, but they should be made non-slip with wire-netting. The logs can form a continuous path or be used in the manner of stepping-stones.

SEATS

Because visitors will almost certainly want to stop by the stream for some time, it is a good idea to provide a seat or two. Use wooden or stone seats that fit in with the natural look. If chosen carefully, a log or flat rock can be comfortable enough for a relatively short stay. Make sure that any seat is placed so that it does not become a dominant feature in its own right.

MATERIALS

Finally, remember that the materials you use are crucial. The rocks and stones you bring to the site should, whenever possible, be those that occur naturally in the local landscape. An outcrop of granite may look imposing, but it will declare its foreignness in sandstone country. Even if no local stone appears naturally close to your garden, the use of a local stone can, on a subconscious level, persuade visitors of the 'rightness' of a feature.

The strata of the rocks in the stream should be aligned, as in nature.

2

Constructing the Pool and Stream

For your stream you need a constant supply of water, and this requires an electric pump to raise it from a reservoir at the lowest level. The reservoir will usually be a pool, but it is equally possible to use a concealed tank should you wish to avoid an area of open water.

It is essential at the outset to establish how you will get the water to the header pool and the electricity to the pump. You will wish to conceal both supplies, probably by burying them under the soil, and the shortest feasible route is to be recommended in order to prevent the great cost and inconvenience involved should you have any problems later on. You will certainly not want to have to excavate a rockery in order to get at a water pipe or electric cable.

PLANNING

Planning plays as important a part in the actual construction of your water feature as in the initial design. If a substantial part of your garden is about to be transformed, consider at a very early stage where you are going to store the necessary equipment and materials. Stone, for example, is heavy, and you should make sure that a long journey is not necessary every time you need another boulder to landscape the stream. It may be convenient to store materials in a corner of the site that will be developed last.

Decide the order in which you are going to tackle the various aspects of the work, and make sure that there are paths between the different areas so that you can move freely with a wheelbarrow. You will probably need help when you move some of the larger pieces of stone, so it is important that any pathways are wide enough to accommodate two people.

You should also consider whether you have adequate vehicular access to your site to permit the removal of waste material and deliveries of stones and rocks. If you decide not to build a rockery with the earth you excavate from the pool and stream, you need to think carefully about what you are going to do with it – you will find that you always take more out of a hole than you expect. It is common courtesy to inform your neighbours in advance of any major work that may affect them. You may, for example, want to take down a common fence to improve access to your site, and the cooperation of those living next door could make your life much easier.

TIMING

Unless you are experienced at this kind of work there will almost certainly be times when delays caused by bad weather, late deliveries and so on will drive you to despair. Develop your stream garden by degrees, allowing more time for each stage than you think will be necessary. Rushing any gardening work is usually a mistake, and this is particularly true when you are creating something as substantial and permanent as a stream garden. You may wish to construct the pond during the first season, progressing to the stream the following year. Even the stream itself can be constructed bit by bit, although you must, of course, start at the bottom so that there is always a channel for the water to run down into the pool.

You might want to consider constructing a stream garden in stages.

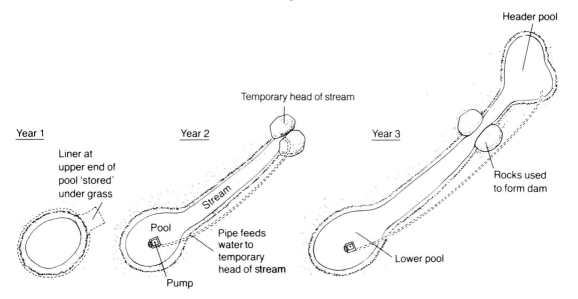

31

DIGGING

You may have little choice about the time of year you carry out the work, although winter, when plants are dormant, is often a good time even though the weather may be unpleasant. Spring may be a better time for the work, but even then there is no guarantee that the rains will not fall just as heavily.

If the work is to be carried out when the soil is wet and heavy, moving it around will be easier if you use planks for the wheelbarrow to ride on. Where the land is uneven rest the planks on stones or bricks or over a raised, firm piece of soil to take the strain, supporting the plank in the middle as well as at the ends. Remember, too, that a loaded barrow is always best pulled up a gradient rather than pushed into it from below. A ricked back at this early stage could ruin all your plans.

Doing-it-yourself does not have to mean that you cannot take advantage of professional help. A small mechanical excavator complete with driver can be hired by the day, and if you can afford it you may be able to get the hardest part of the work completed before you have to start work in earnest yourself.

A few words of warning, though. First, you do need an experienced driver with a feeling for what you are aiming for. Some drivers can manoeuvre diggers with great skill, but remember that, for a natural, restful look, you will probably want curves, which are difficult to sculpt with a machine. Other disadvantages of having a machine are that it may compact the ground in the surrounding area and that, in wet weather, you may be left with deep track ruts to fill.

You will need the following tools and equipment to construct the stream and the pool:

TOOLS

- Hose-pipe (for filling pool and making shape on the ground)
- Spade
- Wheelbarrow
- Planks
- Rake
- Rammer (length of wood for compacting soil and concrete)
- Pegs or bamboo canes (for markers)
- Spirit level
- Long straight edge (length of wood for laying across pegs when taking levels)

EQUIPMENT

- Pond and stream liner
- Underlay
- Concrete mix
- Pump and 25mm (1in) diameter hose
- Electric cable for pump
- Pipes in which to run hose and cable
- Stone for rock features, dams and edging
- Breeze blocks for revetting
- Containers for water plants

Remember that the soil you dig out first will be the most fertile and that you need to retain it for use as topsoil later on. Keep it separate from the other earth you excavate or you will find yourself with a surface in which no self-respecting plant can be persuaded to grow.

CONSTRUCTING THE POOL

You may be planning a series of pools, but the first to be dug out is the one at the lowest part of the garden. It is from here that water will be pumped to the head of the stream; other pools can be added later at a higher level.

If the soil is difficult to work you may be tempted to scrimp on the labour, but the depth of the water will be crucial. For one thing, shallow pools heat up quickly, which is bad for wildlife in general. If you want to keep fish, the pool must be at least 60cm (2ft) deep because they need to be able to submerge to escape from strong sunlight in summer and a possible coating of ice in winter.

Because ice can damage the edges of a pool, it is advisable to slope the sides by at least 20 degrees, which will allow the ice to move up and down without harming the pool sides.

Make sure you leave shelves in your pool 7.5–23cm (3–9in) below the eventual water level. You can either have one continuous ledge or a series of smaller shelves. If the soil is friable and you are planning to use a liner, it is a good idea to cover the shelf or shelves with a light cement screed (a thin, but firm coating) so that they remain firm when the underlay and liner are pulled over them. You should also dig a small trench around the pool, 7.5–10cm (3–4in) from the edge, in which to bury the edges of the liner later on. This trench should be about 15cm (6in) deep.

Remember, too, that you will probably wish to conceal the electric

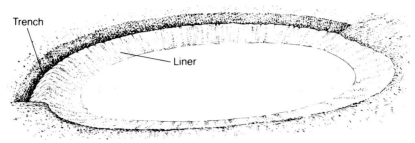

The edges of the pool liner can be concealed in a trench dug a short distance from the pool.

pump inside the pool – under a ledge, perhaps, or beneath foliage. It can be placed on the bottom, but another possibility is to build a shelf for it a little higher up, making access easier when you need to take it out for cleaning.

If the site is flat the soil that is removed can be used to create a raised course for the stream. Otherwise, it is a good idea to use it to build up the ground above the pool to give the impression that the water is lying in a natural hollow.

CHECKING THE LEVEL

When you have finished digging the hole, it is essential to check that the edges are level. Drive in pegs all around the circumference and take bearings using a long straight edge and a spirit level. Correct the levels by building up or lowering the edge as necessary.

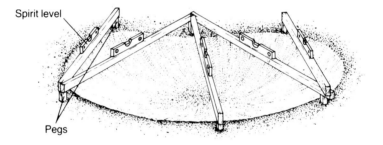

To make certain that the top of the pool is level, drive in pegs around the circumference during construction. Then rest a length of wood on two opposing pegs and work out the respective heights necessary with the help of a spirit level.

TYPES OF LINERS

Having dug out your pool you will have to consider how to line it to prevent the water seeping away. If you have a garden of extraordinarily heavy clay that infallibly retains water you should ram up the puddled clay to create the perfect seal. If you live in a brick-making area you may be able to buy 'blue clay' to line the stream or pool, but the quality can vary so widely that you should adopt this solution only if you are confident of obtaining the very best quality, which will be expensive and, because it is very heavy, difficult to handle.

Pre-formed Pools

One of the easiest solutions as far as the pool is concerned is to use one of the ready-made, rigid fibreglass pools that are available at most garden centres. These come complete with shelves. They are quite expensive, however, and many of them are rather shallow for their surface area. Moreover, although they may have a natural shape and pleasingly curved sides, you will be lucky to find one that is ideal for your particular needs. By all means check what is available, but do not make the mistake of making do with something that will, ultimately, prove unsatisfactory.

PVC and Butyl Liners

The most often used and the most adaptable liners for both pools and streams are sheets of PVC (which may be reinforced), butyl or polythene. Of these, polythene is the cheapest, and it is easy to install. However, it does not stretch as well as the other materials and it has a life of only 1–3 years, especially where it is exposed above ground. PVC is stronger and has a life of 5–10 years; reinforced PVC, though more expensive, is stronger still. Butyl, which is a form of rubber sheeting, is sold either pre-cut in various sizes, or is cut to length from rolls 6m (18ft) or 8m (24ft) wide. It is far stronger and more flexible than either polythene or PVC and, if it is laid correctly, is guaranteed to last for 50 years. It is, as you might expect, the most expensive of the three.

Whichever material you choose, make sure that it is black. This will help to limit the growth of algae by reducing the available light, and it is, in any case, more aesthetically pleasing.

Each of these liners will last longer if it is not exposed to the sun's ultraviolet rays around the edge of the pool. Cover this area with stone, plants, grass or paving.

The liner around the edge of the pool should always be covered so that it is not weakened by the ultraviolet light from the sun. You can use plants, grass, stones or paving.

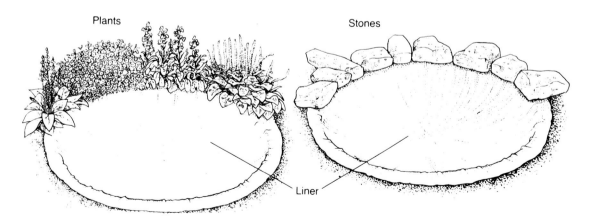

Plants

Stones

Liner

LAYING THE UNDERLAY

The lining fabric will require some form of underlay to protect it against possible puncturing by sharp stones in the soil. A traditional method is to cover the area with very fine sand, obtained from a garden centre or builders' merchants, to a depth of about 2.5cm (1in). The sides of pools and steep streams that are unable to hold the sand can be draped in pieces of old carpets or several layers of wet newspaper. You should hold this material in place with stones until you are ready to lay the liner. In recent years, however, these materials have been superseded by sheets of polyester fibre underlay, which are easy to fit, extremely tough and highly recommended. Small pieces can be cut off to fill awkward corners and gaps and bonded together with a blow torch. Unfortunately this fibre is not cheap, and its use will add to the cost of the project.

Old carpet or layers of wet newspaper will provide a protective underlay for the liner on steep slopes that cannot retain a layer of fine sand.

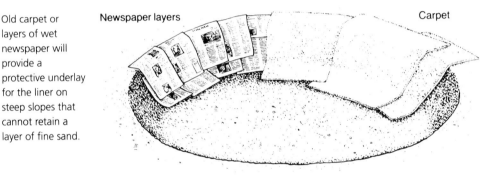

Newspaper layers

Carpet

INSTALLING THE LINER

Before you introduce the liner make sure that all stones and debris have been removed from the surface of the underlay – puncturing the liner will be an expensive mistake. Take care when you carry out this inspection and do not leave ruts and indentations where you have walked: the bottom of the pool must be consistently firm and smooth.

Now you can carefully stretch the liner over the underlay. Allow the middle to touch the bottom first. If the liner comes as a folded strip, lay the strip across the centre of the pool and unfold it from the middle. You will need at least one other person to help you do this, but do make sure that your helpers remove their shoes and walk on the liner as gently and as little as possible. It is at this moment that the additional strength and flexibility of butyl come into their own.

There will inevitably be some folds in the material, and they are not important. Do make sure, though, that there is a good overlap of liner round the edge of the pool. Secure this with stones or other weights.

FILLING THE POOL

As soon as you begin to fill the pool with water you will understand why the overlap was necessary. Start the operation slowly. The weight of the water will alter the stresses on the liner, so while it is filling, adjust the stone weights around the pool as necessary, especially where the liner appears to be stretched too tightly.

You can simply lay the edge of the liner flat over the edge, place firm slabs over it, mortaring them in place, and cut off any surplus. However, this gives a far from natural effect. It is far better to drop the edges of the liner into a small trench (see p. 34) and to cover them with a thick turf. The grass will grow better on a good soil base and will give much better wear.

CONCRETE

The more ambitious gardener may choose to create a concrete pool. This should have a life of 50 years or more, but you must get the techniques right or you may be faced with some extremely expensive mistakes. You should bear in mind, too, that more labour, time and skill are required.

Laying concrete successfully is not impossible, even for those with no experience, but if you are unhappy about mixing it yourself, you can buy bags of ready-mixed concrete that need only the addition of water. In any case, although it may be possible to build your water feature without using concrete, in most instances it will prove to be the ideal material to give stability to dams, rock outcrops, stepping-stones and the walls of the pond. The concrete should be 7.5cm (3in) ballast (sand and stones), used at a ratio of about six parts ballast to one part cement. Some builders would recommend a more costly mix of three to one, to give a hard and longer lasting material. You can incorporate a waterproofing powder into the mix to minimize the possibility of leakage.

In areas that suffer long periods of low temperatures and frost, the sides of the pool should, as with a liner, slope outwards by about 20 degrees so that the water can expand outwards and upwards as it freezes and so reduce the risk of cracking. Such a configuration is more aesthetically pleasing, anyway. You may, however, want to have at least one part of the pool descending vertically because this does give an impression of greater depth. When concreting a slope, use a drier, firmer mix and, if necessary, peg lengths of wood across the slope to hold the concrete while it sets. Afterwards, remove the timber and fill the gaps with concrete.

When you are excavating for a concrete pool, the depth and overall size should be about 15cm (6in) greater than an identical pool with a plastic liner to allow for the thickness of the concrete. Use 500 gauge plastic sheet as a covering before the concrete is laid, 5cm (2in) deep, over the base and up the sides. For a really long-lasting base, reinforcing galvanized wire-mesh can be placed over the first layer of concrete. This should be followed by a further 5cm (2in) layer.

When you are building the wall, gently tamp it down with a rammer every 15cm (6in) or so to force out excess air. Ideally, the bottom and sides should be concreted in a single day, although this cannot be done with a pool that has vertical sides. Here you will have to provide shuttering to hold the wet concrete of the walls until it sets.

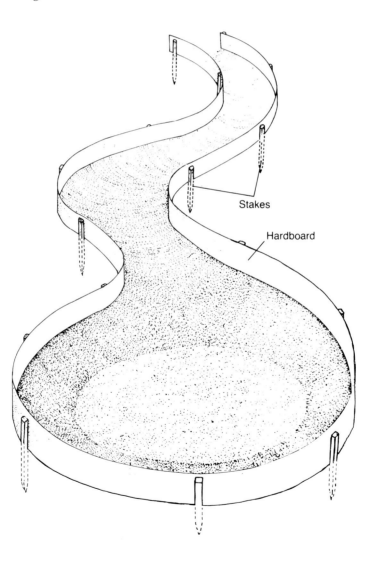

Stakes

Hardboard

Hardboard or plywood, held in place by stakes driven into the ground, is used to shape the stream and pool. The liner can be laid on top of this. Shuttering for the edges of concrete pools can also be secured in this fashion.

An S-shaped stream will make the most of limited space. The pump and connecting pipe are hidden well away from the path and the lawn.

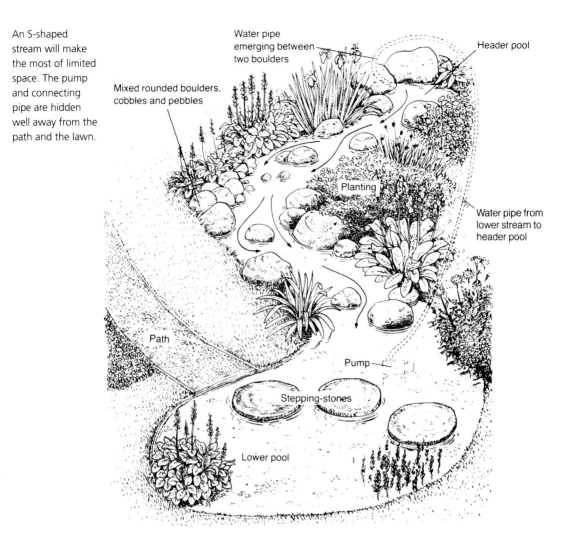

Water pipe emerging between two boulders

Header pool

Mixed rounded boulders, cobbles and pebbles

Planting

Water pipe from lower stream to header pool

Path

Pump

Stepping-stones

Lower pool

Shuttering

Once the concrete of the base has slightly hardened, roughen a strip 15–23cm (6–9in) wide all round the edge to form a key or grip for the side walls. Leave the base to dry for about 48 hours before you start to put in the shuttering. This is like a wooden wall behind which the concrete is poured and it needs to be 5–7.5cm (2–3in) from the edge of the vertical earth wall. The shuttering can be made of standard hardboard. Overlap sheets as necessary and hold them with stout stakes on each side. To prevent bulges forming, you will need to insert stakes in the centre of each sheet of hardboard as well as at the joins. Clearly, it is far easier to build the wall in straight lines, but this is not what is required for a natural-looking pool. The hardboard should, therefore, be bent to give a more natural shape and held in place with stakes.

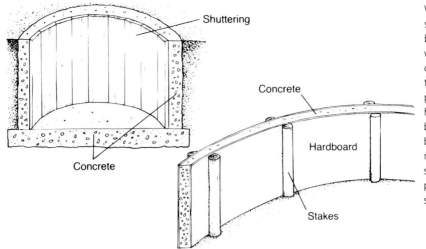

Shuttering

Concrete

Hardboard

Concrete

Stakes

Wooden shuttering acts as a barrier behind which concrete can be poured for the walls of the pool. However, hardboard is better because it can be bent to create a more natural shape. Hold it in position with stakes or pegs.

Before you pour the concrete between the shuttering and the sides of the hole, insert strengthening sections of galvanized wire-mesh or hammer metal rods vertically into the base. It is important to brace the corners. The shuttering can be removed after 2–3 days. Remove sharp edges by rubbing them with a hard stone or a brick and make sure that any holes made between the hard wall and the base, such as where the stakes have been, are filled with concrete.

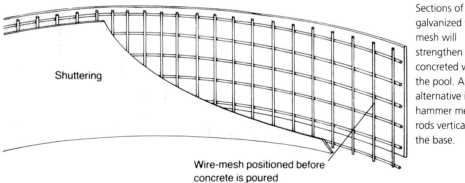

Shuttering

Wire-mesh positioned before concrete is poured

Sections of galvanized wire-mesh will strengthen the concreted walls of the pool. An alternative is to hammer metal rods vertically into the base.

Opposite: Flat stone is ideal for covering the edges of the liner. The colourful *Hosta fortunei* 'Aurea Marginata' in this young stream garden is toned down by the planting of green-leaved hostas.

Concrete Shelving

Shelves and ledges can be formed by creating pockets against the sides, using breeze blocks. Top them with blocks of stone and fill them with well-firmed soil. You can also construct permanent beds for your aquatic plants at this stage by concreting to the bottom building blocks, stones or bricks, and these beds are useful for checking the growth of some of the more vigorous plants. However, if you do not wish to go to that extra trouble, you can always use plastic containers for your water plants.

Right: Breeze blocks, topped by stone to give a natural effect, can be attached to the sides of concrete pools to provide shelves and ledges.

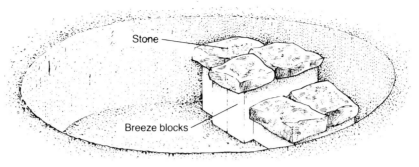

Stone

Breeze blocks

Finishing the Concrete

When the pool is finished, apply a stone-coloured proprietary sealant over the concrete. This will prevent the lime in the cement leaching into the water, which can be harmful to both plants and fish.

However much care you have taken over the shape of your pool, the hard line at the top of the wall will destroy the natural effect unless it

Below: Grass can be grown up to the pool's edge to cover the hard lines of the concrete.

is disguised. You might choose to grow grass up to the edge or over-lap the edge with stone. If you decide to use stone, make a hard core base to bear the weight of the stones and keep them firm.

You should wait at least two weeks before you introduce plants or fish to the pool. This period should allow any alkalinity to level out to pH7.1 or less. You can test the pH level with one of the cheap sets available from garden centres.

LINKING POOLS

When you build your first pool, you may consider that a second pool is likely later on. It is a good idea to extend the liner in the required direction at this early stage, since the channel between the first pool and the proposed second pool, however short, will need to be lined and sealed effectively. You will not want the liner on show, so 'store' it

Right: (Top) Loose stones in the stream bed. Water will travel beneath the stones.
(Bottom) Stones cemented to the stream bed. Water will travel over the top of the stones and some will be held back to create pools.

To construct an overflow, use rocks that vary in size, setting longer stones end on to help hold the smaller rocks in position.

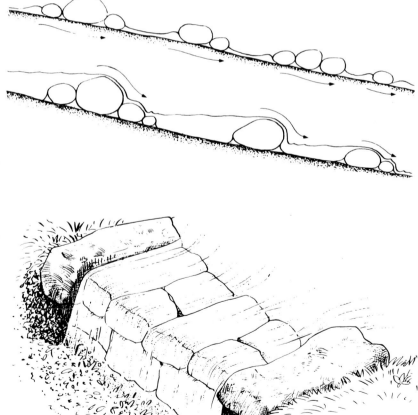

under the turf until you need it. When the second pool has been excavated, retrieve the liner and overlap it with the liner extended from the new pool.

Large, flat stones can be used to hide the liner. Cement them in, using a sealing agent or the water will find its way beneath them – safely above the liner but pointlessly hidden from view. Any rocks that you use should match the rocks around the original pool so that the two seem linked and not two entirely separate entities.

The rocks used in the overflows will look more effective if they vary in size. You can tie them in by using longer stones set end on to hold the others, as happens in the building of a stone wall. If you decide on a single slab, be sure to make it quite level so that the water runs over the full width of it. It is a good idea to gouge a groove under the front end to prevent the water running backwards, out of sight.

PUMPS

There are many models of pump to choose from but only two basic types. Whichever type you select, you must buy the equipment from a

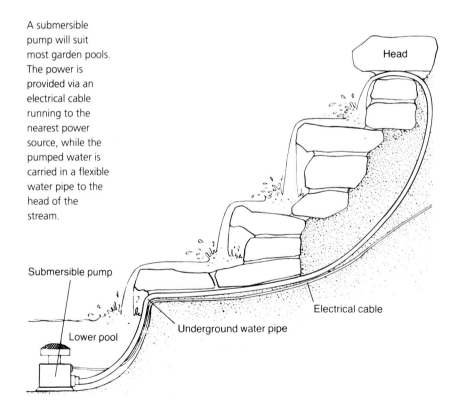

A submersible pump will suit most garden pools. The power is provided via an electrical cable running to the nearest power source, while the pumped water is carried in a flexible water pipe to the head of the stream.

Head

Submersible pump

Lower pool

Underground water pipe

Electrical cable

reputable supplier who will make sure that only approved waterproof connectors are used on the pumps and electrical fittings.

If you are planning a large scheme you can have a surface pump housed in a separate chamber but built at the same time as the pool so that the suction pipe and water intake are incorporated at the same time. If you select this option it is best to have the housing chamber close to the pool but at a lower level so that it is permanently primed.

Most gardeners, however, will opt for a submersible pump, which is adequate for most situations, and we shall assume that this is the type that you are going to use.

The best place for the pump is on bricks or stones at the bottom of the pool, if it is shallow, or on a specially constructed ledge part of the way down. If you are able to position it below a waterfall it will be well hidden from view; otherwise you can camouflage it with plants and stones.

To power your pump you will need an electric cable running back to the nearest power point. Have this installed by a qualified electrician. You might want to consider having the cable in a sunken, reinforced pipe for aesthetic reasons and because it is safer, but do bear in mind that you must be able to get to it in case a fault occurs. It is important to record the routes of cables and to mark the trench where possible. In addition, it is essential to protect the system with a circuit breaker.

You will also need a flexible, 25mm (1in) diameter water pipe to take the pumped water to the header pool. If it will not spoil the look of your stream this can be simply run along the bed. A more natural effect will be achieved, however, if the pipe is run along the ground in a covered trench. If you have a rockery, run the pipe along the soil line rather than beneath the rocks themselves so that it may be easily uncovered if necessary. You can disguise the point of inflow at the pool edge by a flat stone, under turf or something similar. Either run the water pipe through a reinforced pipe or cover it with flat stones or several layers of old polythene bags to protect it from accidental damage. Make sure that the pipe is carefully buried along its whole length, because light will encourage the growth of algae, which could eventually block the pipe.

CONSTRUCTING THE STREAM

As with the excavation of the pool, it is important to keep the fertile topsoil separate if you are digging deeper than a single spit so that it can be used to dress your eventual planting areas.

Opposite: 'Nature abhors a straight line.' Capability Brown's dictum is exemplified by this winding stream, which is enhanced by ornamental planting with *Primula denticulata* and the yellow marsh marigold, *Caltha palustris*.

Do not rush the digging – remember that you are creating a major and probably permanent feature in your garden. You need to be able to stand back and cast a constant and critical eye over your progress. Check that the contours and bends look natural and never hesitate to alter the course if they do not look right.

Remember that sloping sides are stronger than vertical edges. If you have had to build up the course of your stream on otherwise flat ground, consider whether you need a retaining wall to give it permanent stability. You can use something as functional as breeze blocks, mortared with a six to one cement mix, as long as you can disguise it afterwards to retain that all-important natural look.

If you are diverting an existing watercourse, it is vital that you cut any new course before you break into the existing stream. You are building a bypass, which you will fill with water only at the end of your labours.

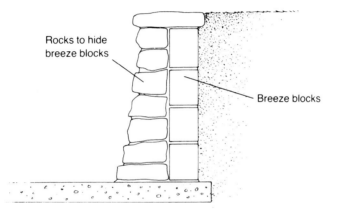

Rocks to hide breeze blocks

Breeze blocks

Breeze blocks can be used to create a retaining wall, but you must disguise them to achieve a natural look.

LINING THE STREAM

The procedures used in digging out and lining the pool apply also to the stream. If the stream is long and meandering you may have to use several strips of butyl lining, and it is vital that there are no escape routes for the running water. Lay the liner at the lower end first, and overlap the succeeding sheets. You can use concrete to line the stream, but this is more expensive and more time consuming, and will not give a natural look.

It is a good idea to run a trench alongside the stream edge, stretching the liner into to it and holding it down with weighty material. The edges of the liner must be firmly covered and well disguised, perhaps

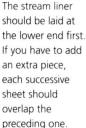

The stream liner should be laid at the lower end first. If you have to add an extra piece, each successive sheet should overlap the preceding one.

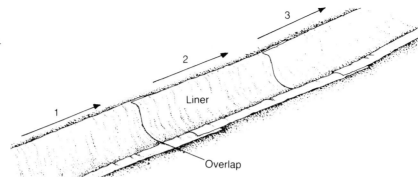

with rocks. Alternatively you could, as with the pool, grow grass right up to the edge of the stream. If you do decide to grass the banks of your stream it is best to use turf at the edges for strength. Lay the turves with the narrow end against the stream (end-on they are firmer and stronger, and people will be walking on them). The rest of the stream area can be seeded if you want a large area of grass, or dug over if you are planning beds and borders.

BUILDING DAMS

Building a dam for a cascade is not a particularly difficult operation, but you will obviously face problems if you try to introduce one to an existing stream with a natural water supply that you cannot simply turn off. In this case you may have to divert the stream while the work is done or put off the job until the drier summer months when the flow may be reduced to a trickle.

If you are starting from scratch you might want to consider throwing up a temporary wooden dam until you are certain of its final position. Make sure that it is set well into the banks on either side or you will lose water around the ends and undermine the banks.

Your permanent dam may be made of wood or of stone. If you choose wood make sure that the timber is of sufficient size and thickness to withstand the constant wear of the water – elm or sweet chestnut are best. Wherever possible use a single piece of timber, and most garden streams will be narrow enough for this to be possible. If your stream is wider, you will need longer lengths and will probably have to support them in the middle. If the stream bed is of clay, you can drive in pegs – not too far, however, for this is only a temporary measure. Pegs will, of course, destroy a liner, and you should use heavy stones, resting them on old pieces of carpet or fibre underlay to protect the liner from damage.

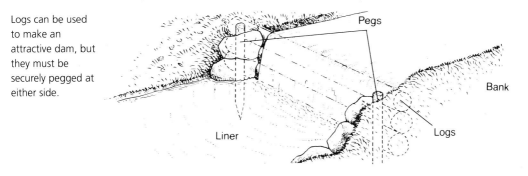

Logs can be used to make an attractive dam, but they must be securely pegged at either side.

Logs placed together and sealed with, for example, clay are not satisfactory, for the clay will move from between the logs. Even using polythene to hold the clay is not a real solution, because water can seep around the end of the polythene, causing the clay to move.

Stone generally makes a more visually interesting dam, although it may be more expensive as you will practically be building a wall. The dam should extend at least 90cm (3ft) into the bank on either side; you will have to cement between the rocks. A cheaper alternative is to erect a concrete dam and face the visible areas with stone. If stone is not available, you could lay logs firmly together lengthways in front of the concrete, pegging them securely at each side, to form an attractive face to the dam over which the water will cascade.

Shuttering

For a concrete dam you will need to erect shuttering of wood or hardboard, as you did for a concrete pool. The shuttering should extend well into the bank on both sides.

Pour in the concrete – a mixture of seven parts ballast to one part cement – and, when it is set, remove the shuttering then face the front and the top with rocks, the larger and fewer the better. These should be cemented, too, for additional stability but this should be done in a manner that is sensitive to the natural appearance of the cascade, with the strata lying horizontally, as in nature.

Erect shuttering of wood or hardboard so that it extends well into the bank on both sides.

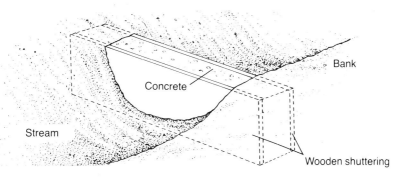

Above: A wide and completely level rim to the basin above produces glistening sheets of falling water.

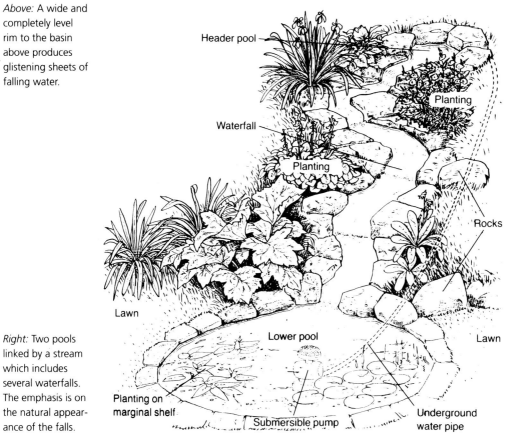

Header pool

Planting

Waterfall

Planting

Rocks

Lawn

Lawn

Lower pool

Right: Two pools linked by a stream which includes several waterfalls. The emphasis is on the natural appearance of the falls.

Planting on marginal shelf

Submersible pump

Underground water pipe

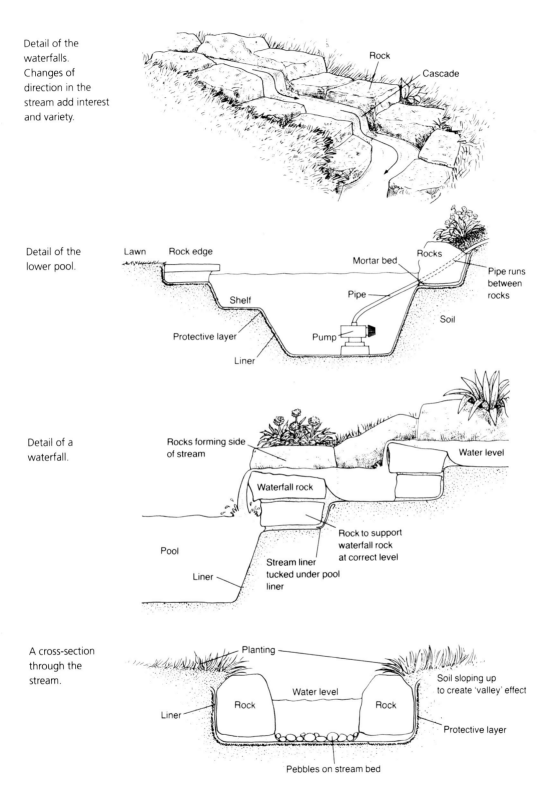

Detail of the waterfalls. Changes of direction in the stream add interest and variety.

Rock

Cascade

Detail of the lower pool.

Lawn

Rock edge

Mortar bed

Rocks

Pipe runs between rocks

Pipe

Shelf

Protective layer

Pump

Soil

Liner

Detail of a waterfall.

Rocks forming side of stream

Water level

Waterfall rock

Pool

Rock to support waterfall rock at correct level

Liner

Stream liner tucked under pool liner

A cross-section through the stream.

Planting

Water level

Soil sloping up to create 'valley' effect

Liner

Rock

Rock

Protective layer

Pebbles on stream bed

The careful placing of the stone at the top is essential because this will affect the flow of water over the cascade. Make sure that it is level, but if you are constructing more than one cascade consider having a wide, even flow for one of them and gaps in the stone to produce a more agitated effect for another.

When the dam is complete it is a good idea to place a large, flat stone on the bed of the stream immediately in front of the cascade or dam, both to prevent the base of the watercourse being scoured out and to produce a lively, splashing effect.

Here advantage is taken of a rock bank to form two pools with a waterfall. The planting pocket and the thick planting around the perimeter will quickly create a natural picture.

Water pipe brought over pool edge in planting area to conceal it

Header pool

Planting

Rockbank

Planting

Water pipe

Pump

Lower pool

Stones on bottom of pool

Planting pocket for marginals

A cross-section of the lower pool. The liner of the lower pool is hidden beneath a turf edge on one side and beneath the liner of the upper pool on the other.

Liner brought up under turf edge

Thin stone to create waterfall

Header pool liner

Large stone cemented to pool base, filled with soil behind

Pump

Soil

Opposite: Moss-covered stone gives the impression of age. A rock below the cascade creates an attractive, splashing effect.

3

Planting the Stream Garden

Once the stream bed has been prepared and the surrounding land contoured, you should give the ground around the stream and the pool a good initial cleaning by digging and forking, then return the topsoil evenly over the surface.

Beds for planting should be well dug, and you should, if possible, incorporate plenty of manure or three-year-old leaf mould. After the digging and levelling, apply a further generous layer of leaf mould or manure, which can be incorporated into the planting holes to reduce the risk of the soil drying out.

Remember that nearly all the species you will plant will stay there for at least three years before they need lifting and dividing, so the soil must be in good condition. If your land is heavy clay, add sand or ashes to open it up.

The actual planting is best achieved by placing all the available plants on the bed in their intended positions, avoiding any straight lines. Start to plant in the middle of the bed, working to the edges and forking out any foot marks as you go. The best effects, both along the stream and in and around the pool, are achieved by grouping plants boldly, but a useful idea to promote a natural appearance is to think of the wind having blown seeds away. Set aside a few plants and, once the group is completed, put the odd one beside the water as if it had escaped from the main planting. We use the word 'odd' advisedly, since experienced gardeners prefer scatterings of three, five or seven to groups of two, four or six. If you happen to have, say, six plants consider grouping five together and placing the sixth a little distance from the rest.

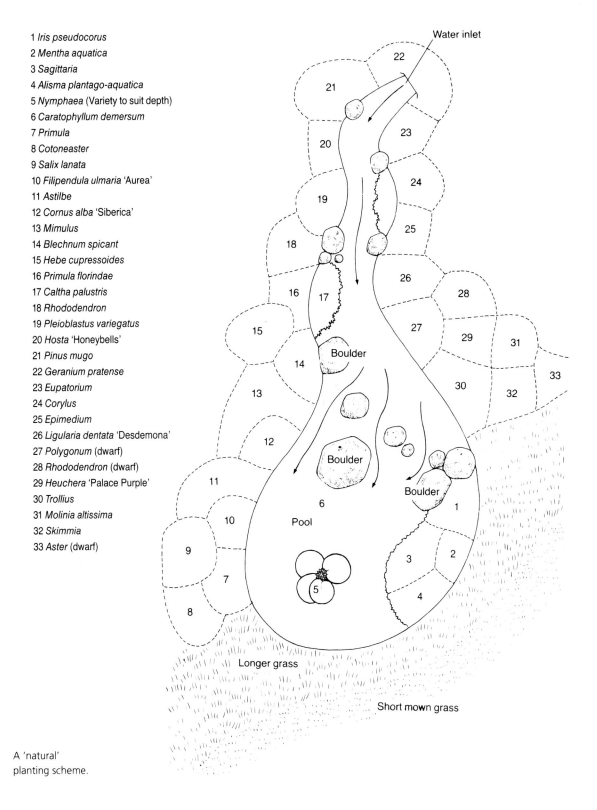

1 *Iris pseudocorus*
2 *Mentha aquatica*
3 *Sagittaria*
4 *Alisma plantago-aquatica*
5 *Nymphaea* (Variety to suit depth)
6 *Caratophyllum demersum*
7 *Primula*
8 *Cotoneaster*
9 *Salix lanata*
10 *Filipendula ulmaria* 'Aurea'
11 *Astilbe*
12 *Cornus alba* 'Siberica'
13 *Mimulus*
14 *Blechnum spicant*
15 *Hebe cupressoides*
16 *Primula florindae*
17 *Caltha palustris*
18 *Rhododendron*
19 *Pleioblastus variegatus*
20 *Hosta* 'Honeybells'
21 *Pinus mugo*
22 *Geranium pratense*
23 *Eupatorium*
24 *Corylus*
25 *Epimedium*
26 *Ligularia dentata* 'Desdemona'
27 *Polygonum* (dwarf)
28 *Rhododendron* (dwarf)
29 *Heuchera* 'Palace Purple'
30 *Trollius*
31 *Molinia altissima*
32 *Skimmia*
33 *Aster* (dwarf)

A 'natural'
planting scheme.

PLANTING DESIGN

It pays to examine the habits, colours and flowering times of each species to produce both harmony and contrast throughout the seasons. Always consider the colours of the plants that are going to be next to each other and also make sure that there is a succession of colour throughout the year. Bulbs, foliage plants and shrubs with colourful bark can provide interest when flowering plants are not in bloom.

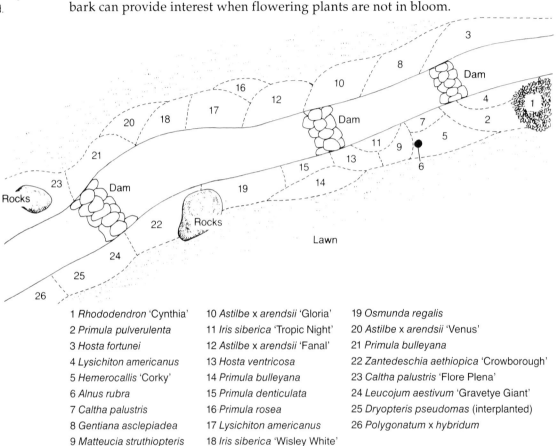

1 *Rhododendron* 'Cynthia'
2 *Primula pulverulenta*
3 *Hosta fortunei*
4 *Lysichiton americanus*
5 *Hemerocallis* 'Corky'
6 *Alnus rubra*
7 *Caltha palustris*
8 *Gentiana asclepiadea*
9 *Matteucia struthiopteris*

10 *Astilbe* x *arendsii* 'Gloria'
11 *Iris siberica* 'Tropic Night'
12 *Astilbe* x *arendsii* 'Fanal'
13 *Hosta ventricosa*
14 *Primula bulleyana*
15 *Primula denticulata*
16 *Primula rosea*
17 *Lysichiton americanus*
18 *Iris siberica* 'Wisley White'

19 *Osmunda regalis*
20 *Astilbe* x *arendsii* 'Venus'
21 *Primula bulleyana*
22 *Zantedeschia aethiopica* 'Crowborough'
23 *Caltha palustris* 'Flore Plena'
24 *Leucojum aestivum* 'Gravetye Giant'
25 *Dryopteris pseudomas* (interplanted)
26 *Polygonatum* x *hybridum*

Spring
In spring you can enjoy the silky, foxy-brown of uncoiling fern fronds, the fresh green foliage of primulas, the rich red of *Rheum palmatum* 'Atrosanguineum', the straight spears of Siberian flag (*Iris sibirica*) and the deep purple shoots of *I.* × *robusta* 'Gerald Darby'. If you have planted daffodils (*Narcissus* species) they will be showing through, perhaps in association with the marsh marigold (*Caltha palustris*) and *Primula denticulata*.

As the water temperature begins to rise in later spring, the red leaves of the water lilies will begin to appear on the surface of the pool. Water hawthorn (*Aponogeton distachyos*) and bog bean (*Menyanthes trifoliata*) will emerge. Yellow skunk cabbage (*Lysichiton americanus*) can be used to provide colour as daffodils begin to die back, and it is particularly attractive when planted in association with the pink-flowering *Primula rosea*.

The grassy, yellow foliage of *Carex elata* 'Aurea' would be an excellent choice for the water's edge, and it would be a wonderful foil for the arum lily (*Zantedeschia aethiopica*); the variety 'Crowborough' is among the hardiest. The summer snowflake (*Leucojum aestivum*) will, despite its name, produce snowdrop-like flowers in spring.

A slowly meandering stream lavishly planted with *Caltha palustris* and *Primula denticulata* for strong, spring colour.

Summer

In summer the plants in and around the pool and stream will provide a wealth of colour and shapes. In the pool itself the first water lily to appear could be the yellow-flowered *Nymphaea* 'Marliacea Chromatella'. It will be followed by *N. alba*, and then *N.* 'Escarboucle', 'Marliacea Carnea', 'Gladstoniana', 'Froebelii' and 'James Brydon'.

At the pool's edges and in the boggy margins of the stream will be the blue flowers of pickerel weed (*Pontederia cordata*) and the contrasting form of the great reedmace (*Typha latifolia*). A spectacular plant for fairly deep water is golden club (*Orontium aquaticum*), which has dark, velvety green leaves, striking white stems and bright yellow flowers. If you have a bog garden, plant *Ligularia dentata*, which grows to 60cm (2ft) and bears vivid orange, daisy-like flowers.

Autumn

Late colour can be provided by crocosmias, easy-growing plants that come into flower late in the summer. They are best planted away from the very wettest areas, but are otherwise not difficult. Try the taller growing, but closely related *Crocosmia paniculata*, which has orange-red flowers on stiff stems and then attractive seedheads, which are popular for autumn and winter flower arrangements. Gentians are usually considered plants for the alpine garden, but the willow gentian (*Gentiana asclepiadea*), so named because of its long, narrow leaves, has graceful, arching stems and bears gentian flowers in the leaf axils in early autumn. This is a plant that will improve with age if it is left alone and not divided. The Kaffir lily (*Schizostylis coccinea*), although not entirely frost hardy, produces crimson flowers in autumn and, unlike the willow gentian, it does benefit from a spring division every few years.

Wildlife haven: this pond, surrounded by *Filipenuda ulmaria*, *Typha latifolia*, *Lythrum salicaria* and *Eupatorium cannabinium*, will attract a host of frogs and newts, birds, butterflies and dragonflies.

Flowers may be relatively few at this time of the year, but the deficiency is not as crucial as it might otherwise be because of the autumn colours provided by foliage and seedheads. Hostas, especially *H. fortunei*, will turn to pleasing shades of yellow, and astilbes, after their summer flowering, will bear still brown seedheads (which should be left on the plant to advantage) while the leaves will take on an attractive bronze-yellow shade.

The shapely fronds of ferns will take on subtle autumn colours, most notably the beautiful royal fern (*Osmunda regalis*) – no water garden should be without this gem. The stems of the striking giant lily (*Cardiocrinum giganteum*), which in summer bore its large, sweetly scented, white flowers, are adorned with shining, dark green seed pods, like small courgettes, in autumn.

Winter

In winter you will find that coloured stems and stalks can add interest to what might otherwise be a dull outlook. When you are planting shrubs such as the red-barked dogwood (*Cornus alba*), *C. stolonifera* 'Flaviramea' with its yellow stems, the orange-stemmed *Salix alba* 'Britzensis' or *Rubus thibetanus* with its distinctive white stems, position them so that you can approach them with the sun behind you. All these plants need to be pruned hard to encourage vigorous young stems. Sweetly scented flowers are rare at this time of year, but *Lonicera × purpusii*, *Viburnum × bodnantense* and *V. × b.* 'Deben' provide this element.

An important aspect to consider is that the plants, however attractive they are, should never totally obscure the water. The play of light on the stream is, after all, one of the special delights of the feature you are developing.

When you buy plants, choose those that are clean, fresh and look vigorous. The largest specimens on offer at nurseries and garden centres are not necessarily the best.

PLANTS FOR THE POOL

Aquatic plants – that is, those plants whose leaves float on the water's surface but that root in the soil at the bottom of the pool, and those plants that float in the water – require deeper water than the marginal plants that thrive in the moist soil at the water's edge.

Although most gardeners will think first of the more colourful deep-water plants – water lilies, water hawthorn and so on – and of the eye-catching marginal plants – such as the sedges (*Carex* species)

Opposite: Invasive growths should be kept in check, leaving areas of open water restful to the eye. Here the large leaves of *Gunnera manicata* form a backdrop for *Astilbe* 'Venus', *Primula helodoxa* and – in the water – *Acorus calamnus variegata.*

and members of the iris family, perhaps – it is vital that the water-cleaning oxygenators are not overlooked, especially if you intend to introduce fish to the pool. These submerged plants help to prevent the build up of ammonia in the water by absorbing waste materials, including the waste products from fish, and converting them into plant protein.

It is important, too, that the introduction of plants, whether aquatic or marginal, is not overdone. Although the surface-leaved plants reduce the amount of light on which the water-greening algae depend, ideally no more than half the water's surface should be covered by surface-floating leaves or the leaves of submerged plants because this will deprive both fish and the plants themselves of much needed light. In addition, if a large area of the surface is covered by leaves, the water loses one of its chief aesthetic functions – its ability to reflect light.

PLANTING THE POOL

After filling your pool with water, wait a week or two before you begin to plant to allow the water to settle. The planting of aquatic species such as water lilies, water hawthorn (*Aponogeton distachyos*) and golden club (*Orontium aquaticum*) and of marginal plants such as reedmace (*Typha* species) and common arrowhead (*Sagittaria sagittifolia*) is best carried out in spring, when plant growth has begun, water temperatures are beginning to rise and there is good light to promote growth. The plants will then have several months in which to build up reserves before the onset of winter weather, and this good start will promote growth and ensure a good display the following season.

In unlined pools – those created on clay, for instance – it may be possible to plant directly into the soil at the bottom, and plants often grow more vigorously in these conditions. A problem may arise when you need to thin these plants out, because they can be difficult to remove without disturbing or damaging the roots.

Aquatic plants are light, and they must be planted firmly. If you have not incorporated permanent beds in your pool, you will have to secure them in basket containers or by means of pegs, wire-netting or stones.

The basket containers that are available from good aquatic nurseries are probably best. They allow water to circulate through the planting medium; they are convenient for thinning because they can be simply lifted out; and they allow you to alter your planting scheme at will by moving the baskets around.

You should line the baskets with hessian to prevent soil loss. Use

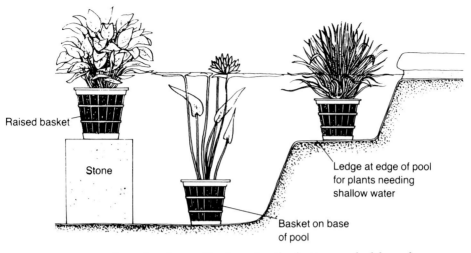

Raised basket

Stone

Ledge at edge of pool
for plants needing
shallow water

Basket on base
of pool

Left: Using containers of plants such as water lilies makes it easy to change your planting scheme. You may find it necessary to place the containers on bricks so that young plants are not in such deep water that they cannot become established.

any good garden loam, the heavier the better, and although you can add a little bonemeal when you first plant the specimens to promote good root growth, you should not use a general fertilizer, which may encourage unwanted, choking leaf growth.

When the baskets are planted, place stones and pieces of turf around the plants on the surface of the compost to act as ballast. Water them well before lowering them into the water to make sure that all the air has been expelled; otherwise dry soil will float away and sink to the bottom.

Whatever plants you introduce, make sure that they are not too deep in the water, especially in the early stages. If they do not receive sufficient light they will die. Planting depths should be measured from the soil level to the water surface, and baskets can be raised on bricks until the plants are established if the water is too deep.

Right: Planting pockets can be introduced at the edge of the pool using blocks, bricks or stone. A rustic-looking alternative can be achieved by using wooden logs.

Opposite: This mature stream garden illustrates the value of foliage, with its various shapes, shades and textures.

PLANTS FOR THE STREAM

The boggy edges of the stream are ideal for plants that enjoy having their feet in the water, and in many cases these will be the same species that you will introduce to the pool – bog bean (*Menyanthes trifoliata*), yellow flag (*Iris pseudacorus*) or water plantain (*Alisma plantago-aquatica*), for example. However, many garden plants thrive in moist soil, and although you should not position such species as astilbes, hostas and primulas where their roots will be permanently in water, there will be many places near the stream where such plants can be successfully grown.

There is a wide variety of plants for use along the margins of a stream. In general it is best to follow a bold and simple planting

scheme, with contrasts of form as well as colour. The sturdy foliage of hostas such as *Hosta ventricosa* or *H. fortunei*, for example, will emphasize the delicate filigree of the royal fern (*Osmunda regalis*), the ostrich fern (*Matteuccia struthiopteris*) or that plumiest of ferns, the soft shield fern (*Polystichum setiferum*).

Opposite: A dense planting of the royal fern, *Osmunda regalis*, with *Iris siberica* at the water's edge.

In a similar fashion, the sword-shaped leaves of the Siberian flag (*Iris sibirica*) will provide a contrast to the round foliage of *Ligularia dentata* or the graceful foliage and flowers of astilbes. In a larger garden the huge leaves of gunnera can be exaggerated by the presence of a tall grass such as *Miscanthus sinensis*. The brilliant yellow of the skunk cabbage (*Lysichiton americanus*) will be a focal point when in flower and will look especially pleasing when planted so that it is reflected in the water.

When you are preparing your planting scheme you need to imagine how the features will look when they are complete and fully stocked. You will, no doubt, wish to have plants clustered alongside the water in many places, but you should consider creating open areas where your lawns run down to the stream. You can guide your visitors to the most eye-catching spots by designing such approaches at the early stages.

In the same way you should visualize where the plants will be grouped. They will have the greatest impact if they are on the far side of the stream from where your visitors will stand or sit. You might want to consider widening the stream in such areas, forming shallow ledges for plants that enjoy boggy conditions. Taller plants should be allowed to colonize the lower levels, with smaller specimens higher up, so that you avoid a top-heavy look. Shrubs, especially the willows (*Salix* species) and dogwoods (*Cornus* species), will not only provide year-round colour but will help to consolidate the banks. Some suitable species are listed in the Plant Directory (see p. 80).

When revetting is used on the edge of a stream or pool, its hard lines can be softened by overhanging stone and the introduction of plants that spill over the edge.

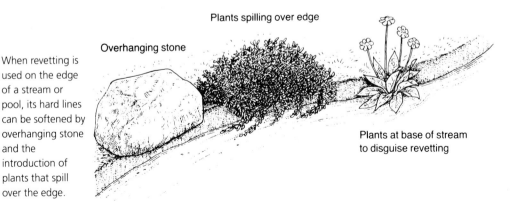

Plants spilling over edge

Overhanging stone

Plants at base of stream to disguise revetting

4

Case Studies

The two stream gardens described in this chapter are very different –
one is an ordinary suburban garden while the other is in a large,
already landscaped park – but they both illustrate how the design and
construction principles discussed in Chapters 1 and 2 can be put into
practice when creating a stream garden.

A SUBURBAN GARDEN

This was a particularly challenging project for the garden designer
since the site had no natural water and it was a flat, rather uninterest-
ing back garden – the least likely setting imaginable for a 'natural'
water feature.

When the designer first saw the plot it had been used almost exclu-
sively for vegetable growing and was littered with cabbage and brus-
sels sprout stumps. It was a fairly large, north-facing area, measuring
14 × 30m (46 × 90ft).

Close to the house on the west side was a 3.4 × 4m (10 × 12ft) greenhouse, and beyond that lay an old concrete pond. The garden, open at
the north end, was divided from its neighbouring plots by a line of
small trees along the western side and a well-maintained beech hedge
to the east.

The topsoil was generally good, having been regularly dressed with
compost and calcified seaweed to combat acidity and to supply trace
elements for vegetables. The subsoil, however, was clay with flints
and rather poor.

It is not easy to see the potential of a drab, flat and uninspiring suburban plot such as this. This was the site immediately before work began.

THE BRIEF

The owners wanted the water feature to form only a small part of the whole area – most of the western part of the area was to be given over to vegetable growing. It was also decided to leave the greenhouse near the house, where it received maximum light, especially in winter.

The old pond was to be removed. A new pool was to be installed at the northern end of a terrace that would connect the stream garden area to the house. The pool would be stocked with fish, although these would not be exotic varieties but fish that would be in keeping with the local environment and would fend for themselves in the depth of water provided and ambient temperatures.

The owners wanted to introduce the sound of water to their garden and hoped to encourage wildlife, but their prime concern was that it would be a low-maintenance garden.

INITIAL PLANNING

The owners had allowed a full year to elapse between the initial decision to construct a stream garden and starting work. During that time they had placed poles in the ground to show which areas caught the sun at different times of the day and year and noted where the wind blew fallen leaves. They decided to begin work after the worst of the winter weather was over, hoping that it could be completed in a couple of months.

THE FORMAL PLAN

The garden designer sought to overcome two potential problem areas – the places where the formal area around the house met the natural-ness of the water feature and where the recreational part of the garden met the working area.

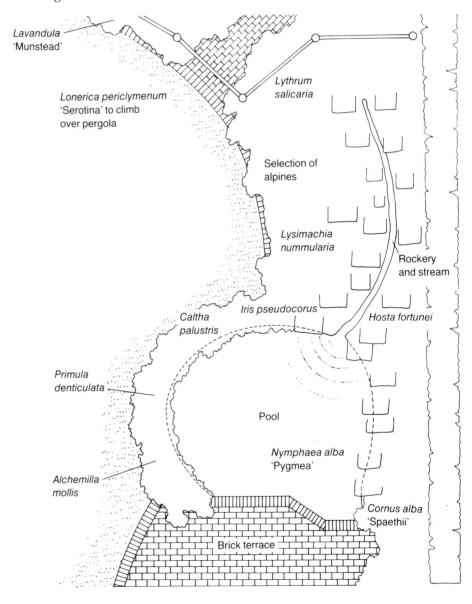

Lavandula 'Munstead'

Lonerica periclymenum 'Serotina' to climb over pergola

Lythrum salicaria

Selection of alpines

Lysimachia nummularia

Rockery and stream

Iris pseudocorus

Caltha palustris

Hosta fortunei

Primula denticulata

Pool

Nymphaea alba 'Pygmea'

Alchemilla mollis

Cornus alba 'Spaethii'

Brick terrace

Plan of the new garden.

It was decided that the stream garden would be close to the beech hedge on the eastern side. Space was limited, so a single pool was chosen, fed through a short stream winding between rocks. Water would enter the head of the stream through a concealed pipe, and although the fall from the top of the rockery to the bottom would be only about 60cm (2ft), it would mimic in miniature the aspects of a natural environment, from drier upper slopes to boggy lowlands.

The sitting area around the pool needed to be some way from the house in order to catch the sun, and it was decided to place it at the end of a brick terrace so that the water feature would seem to be almost an extension of the house, although the bricks would be separated from the stone of the rockery by planting. The brickwork, used as a unifying device, was formal nearer to the house and became less detailed closer to the pool.

A pergola would screen the upper part of the vegetable garden from the water area, but an arch to one side would offer a teasing enticement to something unseen beyond it. Access to the vegetable plot would also be via a small herb garden opposite the sitting area, thus encouraging movement around the whole garden by a number of possible routes.

Although the water feature was to be positioned close to the sitting area, it was planned to be seen from all around the garden. The bog garden, along one side of the stream, was to be divided by a small, open area of lawn so that visitors could walk to the water's edge.

The design was guided as much by practical as by aesthetic considerations – the route from the house for the water and electrical supplies, for example. The creation of a rockery next to the pool, a desirable feature in itself, is an efficient use of the excavated earth.

MATERIALS

The stone for the garden was obtained from a sandstone quarry a few miles from the garden. The designer visited the quarry and was able to select exactly the right mixture of flat stones for the water to run across and tall ones for the rockery. The stones chosen had occasional bluish tinges, which echoed the blue in the bricks that were to be used. Despite the small area covered by the stream garden, 11 tonnes (or tons) of rocks were required.

The project also needed a small number of hollow, 23cm (9in) concrete blocks, which were used to build the retaining walls between the eastern side of the feature and the beech hedge, which would prevent soil spilling through to the neighbour's garden, and around the highest part of the stream bed, which needed firm support.

These blocks were used instead of dry stone walling, which would have been much more expensive, but they needed to be hidden. The wall by the hedge would be out of sight, and it was decided to camouflage the others with sweet chestnut poles, which would fit well with the pergola. Sweet chestnut is tolerant of wet conditions, but although the poles themselves would have provided a firm retaining wall, it was felt that they would not last as long as the water feature itself without becoming unstable.

The other materials needed were heavy-duty black butyl lining and felt underlay for both stream and pool. A submersible electric pump would be installed in the pool to pump water to the head of the stream through a tough, clear, 25mm (1in) alkythene pipe. The electric cable would also be contained in a plastic pipe.

CONSTRUCTING THE POOL

A mechanical digger was hired for the initial excavation of the pool, which took half a day; digging out the pool by hand would probably have taken several days. The driver was told to dig out a rough shape to a depth of 90cm (3ft), leaving the rest to be modelled by hand.

Half the topsoil was spread over the vegetable plot and the other half was piled near to the greenhouse, for later use on the surface of the stream garden. The flint-ridden subsoil was thrown above the pool and would be used to form the raised bed of the stream.

The old pond was dug out, the concrete removed from the site and the ground filled in and flattened.

Shaping the Pool

Several distinct levels in the pond were marked by dustings of coarse sand. A ring of bamboo canes inside the pool showed the intended water level. There was to be a shelf about 45cm (18in) above this on which rocks would be placed, the idea being that they would seem to spill down into the water, with one or two actually sitting on the planting shelf.

There were to be two shelves below the water line: a shallow planting shelf about 7.5cm (3in) down and a broad shelf 60cm (2ft) down for the pump and water lilies. In a shallow pool, the pump and water lilies could sit on the pool floor; at 90cm (3ft), however, this pool would be too deep for this. The pool was to have a straight edge where it met the paving of the terrace so that the liner or planting shelf could not be seen by visitors looking down into the water, which would appear to be very deep.

As the pool neared completion it became obvious that the water

level must not be allowed to deviate by even the smallest amount, for the slightest slope would reveal the black liner above the water line and ruin the effect. The designer used an instrument known as an SL10, which has a telescope eyepiece with cross hairs on it and which can be hired by the day. The alternative method is to hammer pegs around the pool, lay boards across them and check with a spirit level (see p. 34).

(see p. 34).

The soil around the 'sculpted' pool is dressed with a light render for strength. The ledges are for plants which require different depths of water.

Rendering the Pool

Giving the pool its final shape took two days. The flinty soil tended to break away at crucial times and required continual making-good. When they had been shaped, the sides and bottom of the pool were lightly rendered with a mixture of six to one sand and cement. This would not have been necessary with a firm, clay soil, but the smooth screed gave the walls more stability and ensured that the liner would not be damaged by any protruding flints.

Fitting the Underlay

Because the edges of the shelves were now sharp and rather well defined, they were rounded off by vigorous brushing with a broom before the underlay was put down. The underlay further softened the edges of the shelves. The underlay has a rather clinging effect, which helped in the fitting, and any gaps were filled with small pieces, which were bonded with a blow torch.

Before the liner was fitted the underlay was carefully inspected to check that no small stones had fallen into the pool during the work. Such stones, trapped between liner and underlay, could easily cause damage to the liner.

Improvised
material such as
carpets or old
newspapers can be
used on a bed of
fine sand as
underlay to protect
the liner, but
polyester fibre
underlays have the
advantage of
clinging to the soil.

Fitting the Liner

Two people, working in stockinged feet, fitted the liner. Because the pool had a rather irregular shape it was impossible to avoid folds occurring, but these were considered unimportant as they could be hidden beneath rocks. The liner protruded above the pool's edge all round, where it would be later held in place by soil and rocks. It was vital that a good length of liner was left extending towards the eventual watercourse, where it would be overlapped by the stream liner.

Along the terrace edge of the pool the liner would come up under the first line of bricks and be lost behind it, while in the bog garden and grassed area it would be brought up and buried in a trench.

CREATING THE STREAM BED

The most time-consuming task was the building of the rockery that was to form the bed of the stream. Not only were the stones extremely heavy, but placing them required great aesthetic judgement.

The rough course of the stream, winding from the northeast corner of the water feature, had been agreed, and work began at the point at which it fell into the pool. A length of liner (with underlay) was spread across the soil along the route of the watercourse, overlapping the liner of the pool. Three lengths of liner were required for the stream, each section of liner overlapping the one below and sealed and hidden by rocks.

Two large stones were chosen to be butted together on the planting shelf, their tops just above the water. Above them, and lying partly across them, was a flat stone over which the water would glisten as it ran.

The pool and stream liners overlapped between the flat stone and the one behind it, and a waterproof sand and cement mortar was added here. The water would fill the gap between the two stones, completely hiding the gap, which would be further disguised by algae and a few scattered stones.

The detailed course of the stream depended on the available rocks and their positioning. Because of their great weight and the quantity – 70 were used in all – careful thought was given to the design. Size was important, because the rocks had to fit together and to take the water by stages downstream, but it was also vital that the rocks mimicked the natural features, with collapsed rocks beneath larger ones and the strata in the same direction.

The designer's advice was: 'When you change direction, step it round the corner, rather than twisting the rock. And make sure that the face of the rock is in the best place to be seen. These rocks are quite expensive, and you don't want to bury them in the ground so that they are hidden from view. '

Although the feature was too small for dramatic cascades, care was taken to position the rocks so that the water meandered down over a few miniature falls, both to make it more interesting and to exaggerate the sound of running water.

The pool and stream with all the rocks in place. The liner protruding between the bricks in the foreground would later be concealed beneath the top layer of bricks.

Just as the exact course of the stream was unknown at the beginning of the work, so it was impossible to predict exactly where the pockets of soil between the rocks would be. Because the choice of plants would depend to some extent on the size and position of these pockets, it would have been a mistake to decide definitely about the planting in advance.

In addition to the rocks at the end of the stream, several were placed in and around the pool to suggest a natural rock formation rising from under the water. These were fixed to the liner with a waterproof sand and cement mortar, with the lower ones resting on the pool shelves.

The plastic pipe for pumping water from the pool to the head of the stream was hidden in the ground at the foot of the rockery so that it could be uncovered in case of problems. At the top of the stream it was hidden by two rocks, and its end was cut at an angle so that the water flowed gently down rather than spurting out.

Early days in the stream garden. The winding course of the stream is not only attractive in its own right, but makes good use of the limited space.

PLANTING THE GARDEN

When the rockery was completed the topsoil from the excavated pool was used to dress the plant pockets. This was supplemented by bought-in topsoil and compost from the garden. Bonemeal was applied as a slow-release fertilizer.

One of the aims of the planting was to disguise part of the water feature from the herb garden so that visitors would be enticed forwards to get a better view of the stream. The spread of plants over the rock face, by taking the eye from the hard edges of the stone, would have the effect of making those areas seem larger than they really are.

The Bog Garden

Only a submerged line of bricks (camouflaged by encroaching plants) separated the bog garden from the grass beyond, but the lower ground close to the pool allowed a choice of plants that would tolerate very wet conditions.

Purple loosestrife (*Lythrum salicaria*) was planted in the boggy area closest to the house, its height helping to frame the pond as seen from the terrace and so enclose the area. It also balanced the height of the hedge on the other side of the garden. Creeping Jenny (*Lysimachia nummularia*) was used for ground cover. Further around the pond, in the boggy area seen from the vegetable garden, yellow mimulus (*Mimulus glutinosa*), the drumstick primula (*Primula denticulata*), the showy marsh marigold (*Caltha palustris*) and *Iris laevigata* 'Variegata' were planted.

The first spring in the new stream garden and the planting is already encroaching over the rock surfaces. The blue of *Brunnera macrophylla* contrasts with the yellow of the marsh marigold, *Caltha palustris*.

The Pond

The yellow flag (*Iris pseudacorus*) was planted in the pond to the right of the terrace to balance the height of the purple loosestrife. Other pond plants included the flowering rush (*Butomus umbellatus*) and the water hawthorn (*Aponogeton distachyos*). Further colour was provided by the red water lily *Nymphaea* 'James Brydon'.

Marginal Planting

The various areas surrounding the stream were treated differently. Smaller plants, including a white astilbe and a hosta, were introduced immediately north of the pond, allowing the rocks and stream to be seen from the vegetable garden.

Screen planting was introduced behind the stream garden to hide that part of the vegetable garden and foreshorten the view. Several dogwoods (*Cornus alba* 'Elegantissima') were planted there, their red stems providing vivid winter colour.

The area in front of the beech hedge was given a taller planting in shades of whites and yellows as a background to the stream garden – *Ligularia przewalskii* 'The Rocket', dropwort (*Filipendula vulgaris*) and a white *Astilbe* × *arendsii*.

Tree trunks and branches are reflected in the water in this stream garden at Sheffield Park. Dams of rock and wood were introduced to emphasize the different levels of the garden.

SHEFFIELD PARK

The beautiful woodland garden at Sheffield Park in Sussex covers approximately 40 hectares (100 acres). It is planted with an internationally recognized collection of trees and shrubs, including almost two hundred species of conifer and a large collection of azaleas and rhododendrons. Water is one of the site's greatest assets. The great British landscape designer Lancelot 'Capability' Brown (1716–83) created two of the garden's four large lakes, but there was space away from his design that lent itself to the incorporation of a new feature that would not intrude on the former landscaping.

In another area of the Sheffield Park stream garden *Hosta fortunei* is in flower, close to the shuttlecock fern, *Matteuccia struthiopteris*, with a bold clump of the large-leaved *Gunnera mancata* in the background.

THE BRIEF

The purpose of this new feature was to increase the plant collection and extend the period of interest and also to encourage visitors to spread out, thus reducing the wear on the central part of the garden. The site chosen was a dip in the land, and the whole area, which was a piece of rough woodland on the boundary, was initially covered in bracken and brambles with a few oak and ash trees, but nothing more.

INITIAL PLANNING

When the fence was removed and bracken cleared, a little ditch, about 30cm (1ft) wide, was found; it carried the drainage water from the

A ribbon effect should be avoided in stream-side planting. On the far side of this section of the stream only the yellow-flowering *Lysimachia punctata* borders the water, whereas the near side is dense with a variety of plants.

field above down to the large lake. The potential for the area as a stream garden was not immediately obvious, but when the ditch was cleaned out, some dams were added to hold some of the water back to create pools that would reflect light. The original dams were constructed of oak and later on more permanent dams, made of local stone, were constructed. The ditch was widened and the sides dug out to create a gently meandering stream. A simple wooden bridge – designed to blend in with its surroundings – was then added.

The guiding principle was that nothing should seem to be contrived, and plants were added as the stream garden evolved. The beauty of the project was that it really involved very little work at all. The construction was undertaken gradually, a little each winter, for parks such as this can no longer justify the large numbers of staff that would be needed for intensive work on any one feature.

DEVELOPING A PLANTING SCHEME

Two principles underlay the planting decisions: low-maintenance and the need to provide colour in Sheffield Park after the rhododendrons and azaleas had flowered.

To reduce the labour of cutting the banks of grass beside the stream, this area was planted with ground-cover subjects – chiefly hostas, astilbes, ferns and Siberian flag (*Iris sibirica*) – to add interest and colour. Hostas and astilbes were selected partly because they are so easy to increase by division, while the sword-shaped leaves of Siberian flag form a wonderful contrast with the hostas. In addition to

Hosta fortunei 'Aurea', two cultivars, 'Honeybells' and 'Royal Standard', were introduced to extend the flowering season and to bring diversity of leaf colour.

Apart from the royal fern (*Osmunda regalis*), there are large plantings of the ostrich (or shuttlecock) fern (*Matteuccia struthiopteris*). When the fronds appear in early spring, they are shaped just like a shuttlecock.

The only plant that was already growing beside the stream was the giant gunnera (*Gunnera manicata*), which is a wonderfully architectural plant but is not suitable for a small garden. The leaves can be up to 1.5m (5ft) across, and the plants will grow to 1.8m (6ft) high or more. These plants will thrive in marshy ground.

Some of the plants were deliberately placed in the water rather than on the bank, to give the effect of having seeded themselves. Some ferns and primulas actually grow in the water, while a little further down the stream yellow skunk cabbage (*Lysichiton americanus*) has been planted.

The importance of keeping open stretches of water was recognized, and a conscious effort was made to limit the planting in some areas so that the reflections in the water were not lost. This is a principle that is as relevant to the small stream garden as to the large – it is all too easy for enthusiastic gardeners to obscure the water by overplanting.

The larger garden can achieve grand effects, as here at Sheffield Park, where the red of the foreground *Primula pulverulenta* is echoed by the rhododendron beyond the lawn.

5

Plant Directory

The plants contained in this directory are divided into ten groups. The first five groups – water plants, submerged oxygenators, floating plants, marginal plants and moisture-loving plants – contain those plants that you should introduce into the pool itself and along its margins and the edges of the stream. The remaining groups – ferns, bulbs, grasses, trees and shrubs – include plants that thrive in damp soils and that can be planted elsewhere in the stream garden to provide year-round colour and interest. Most of the plants in these five groups will tolerate a wide variety of soils, provided they are moisture-retentive, and they do not require artificial fertilizers if you can give them some humus when you plant them. Most plants benefit from bonemeal, however, which encourages root growth.

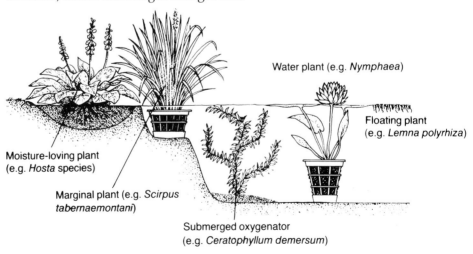

Water plant (e.g. *Nymphaea*)

Floating plant
(e.g. *Lemna polyrhiza*)

Moisture-loving plant
(e.g. *Hosta* species)

Marginal plant (e.g. *Scirpus tabernaemontani*)

Submerged oxygenator
(e.g. *Ceratophyllum demersum*)

Water-loving plants and their environment.

WATER PLANTS

This group includes those plants that will grow with their roots entirely submerged in water and with their leaves floating on the water's surface.

APONOGETON DISTACHYOS (WATER HAWTHORN, CAPE PONDWEED)

Native to South Africa but now naturalized in western Europe, South America and northern Australia, this species has fragrant, white flowers with distinctive black anthers. The strap-like leaves grow to 25cm (10in) long. It will thrive in water from 15 to 60cm (6–24in) deep, and, if kept in a disciplined group, water hawthorn will eventually make quite an impressive show.

HOTTONIA PALUSTRIS (WATER VIOLET)

Found throughout temperate areas of the northern hemisphere, this floating plant could be included in the list of oxygenating plants, for the whorls of fern-like, light green leaves remain under water. The spikes of pretty pale mauve flowers, however, are borne about 15cm (6in) above water in early summer. Simply drop the plant into the water, where it will establish itself.

The water violet, *Hottonia palustris*, with its lilac and white flowers, needs to be fully submerged in the water.

MENYANTHES TRIFOLIATA (BOG BEAN, BUCKBEAN)

A native to northern temperate countries, this species has mid-green leaves, which are similar to those of the common broad bean and are borne in threes on a single stem. It is one of the food plants of the larvae of the elephant hawk moth and is, therefore, a useful addition to a wild garden. The pretty white flowers, which appear in early spring and are borne in spikes to 23cm (9in) high, have purple stamens and a pinkish fringe; the buds are pink. It will grow in water 5–10cm (2–4in) deep but is also a good marginal subject. It will need to be reduced occasionally.

NYMPHAEA (WATER LILY)

The water lily is the most exotic addition to any pool. Good-quality plants can be expensive, but these aristocrats of the water garden seldom need replacing once they are established, and they will flower faithfully summer after summer. There are many varieties to choose from, including some small cultivars that are suitable for limited areas of water. Those listed here are, inevitably, just a selection of some of the most reliable. These water lilies are hardy, but they do require a good period of sunshine each day if they are to flower well, or they will produce foliage at the expense of blooms. However, the shade of the leaves does help to control the growth of algae. Water lilies need still water and should not be sited where the leaves will be directly under the spray from a fountain or waterfall. There is, unfortunately, a great deal of confusion in the naming of the different cultivars, and many are sold under the wrong names. If possible, buy your water lilies from a reputable nursery or garden centre and try to obtain plants that are already in flower in order to avoid later disappointment.

N. alba
This native to lakes and slow-moving rivers of Europe has green leaves and fragrant, white, golden-centred flowers, which can be up to 10cm (4in) across. Grow it in water to 90cm (36in), although it has been known to survive in water to 1.2m (4ft) deep. It is generally too vigorous for all but the largest pools.

N. 'Albatross'
Suitable for water 23–45cm (9–18in) deep, this is not as vigorous as *N. alba*. However, the snow-white flowers are a pretty shape and contrast beautifully with the apple-green leaves.

N. 'Amabilis' ('Pink Marvel')

The star-shaped, salmon-pink blooms, up to 25cm (10in) across, are borne amid deeply cut, dark green foliage. It is suitable for water 30–75cm (12–30in) deep.

N. 'American Star'

A vigorous, eye-catching variety, it has freely borne, star-shaped, pink flowers, which are delicately scented. The leaves are dark green. Grow it in water 23–60cm (9–24in) deep.

N. 'Attraction'

This free-flowering variety, which needs water 38–90cm (15–36in) deep and as much space as possible, has red petals, flecked with white, which deepen to dark red with age. The flowers are 20–25cm (8-10in) across.

N. 'Conqueror'

Grown in water 23–60cm (9–24in) deep, this is an attractive, free-flowering variety. Young foliage is purplish, turning green as it ages. The large, red flowers remain open in the evening.

N. 'Escarboucle'

Another variety to be grown in water 23–60cm (9–24in) deep, this is a popular and reliable water lily. The star-like blooms are a brilliant crimson, which deepens with age. The foliage becomes reddish later in the year.

N. 'Froebelii'

The cup-shaped, fragrant, blood-red flowers of N. 'Froebelii' have bright vermilion stamens with yellow anthers, and the leaves are green. It has a fairly limited spread and should be grown in water 15–23cm (6–9in) deep.

N. 'Gladstoniana'

The semi-double, white, star-shaped flowers are 15–30cm (6–12in) across and make this one of the most beautiful of the white-flowered water lilies. It will grow in water 38–90cm (15–36in) deep and can be vigorous.

N. 'Marliacea Carnea' ('Marliac Flesh', 'Morning Glory')

The star-shaped flowers, 20cm (8in) across, are a very pale pink and the leaves are green. It is a free-flowering and vigorous variety, which needs water 30–75cm (12–30in) deep.

N. 'Marliacea Chromatella' ('Golden Cup')

This dependable variety has large, yellow flowers, 15cm (6in) across, which stay open later in the day than those of many other water lilies. The attractive foliage is mottled and spotted with reddish-brown blotches. Grow it in water 30–75cm (12–30in) deep. It will tolerate some shade.

N. 'Sioux'

When they open the flowers of this lily are pale yellow; then they turn orange; finally they become a warm, copper red. The bronze-green leaves are attractively mottled with dark brown. This is a suitable variety for a small pool and should be planted in water 23–45cm (9–18in) deep.

ORONTIUM AQUATICUM (GOLDEN CLUB)

Native to eastern North America, this is an attractive plant. It has dark green leaves with a silvery sheen and bears gold and white, pencil-like flower spikes in spring. It grows 23–25cm (9–10in) high. It prefers deep water, at least 30cm (12in), although it will grow, though less vigorously, as a marginal subject, but it does require at least 15cm (6in) of soil or mud for its roots.

SUBMERGED OXYGENATORS

Oxygenating plants are submerged, rootless, fast-growing plants that dissolve mineral salts that would otherwise promote the growth of algae. They are, therefore, essential features of every pool. One dozen for every 7.5sq m (24sq ft) of water surface is recommended.

CALLITRICHE VERNA (SYN. C. PALUSTRIS) (STARWORT)

Native to countries throughout the northern hemisphere, this pretty, pale green foliage plant is not easy to establish. The plant will die down in the winter. Its relative *C. autumnalis* has the advantage that it continues to grow throughout the winter months.

CERATOPHYLLUM DEMERSUM (HORNWORT)

This hardy, undemanding species is found throughout the world. It has dense whorls of feathery, dark green foliage, which creates an ideal environment for fish.

Opposite:
Nymphaea
'Marliacea
Chromatella' is still
one of the best
yellow water lilies.

FONTINALIS ANTIPYRETICA (WILLOW MOSS, WATER MOSS)

Native to temperate countries in the northern hemisphere and also to southern Africa, this fully hardy plant will tolerate sun or partial shade. It will grow in still water but prefers running water, and it forms dense patches of dark green leaves. *Fontinalis antipyretica* reaches a height of 2.5cm (1in), and the spread is indefinite.

LAGAROSIPHON MAJOR (SYN. ELODEA CRISPA)

Although it is native to South Africa, this spreading plant is naturalized in Europe and New Zealand and is one of the most often seen oxygenating plants. The slender stems are covered with dark green leaves, and it forms dense clumps of foliage. It bears insignificant flowers in summer. Choose it in preference to the even more vigorous *Elodea canadensis* (Canadian pondweed).

MYRIOPHYLLUM AQUATICUM (SYN. M. PROSERPINACOIDES) (PARROT'S FEATHER)

Despite its wide distribution throughout the northern hemisphere, this spreading plant is not fully hardy, and if you can, keep some indoors in a suitable container in winter. It has finely divided, bluish-green foliage, which turns reddish in autumn if it is on the surface, and it is ideal for camouflaging unsightly pool edges.

POTAMOGETON CRISPUS (CURLED PONDWEED)

Found throughout Europe and Asia, this submerged plant resembles seaweed. It forms spreading colonies of wavy-edged, bronze or mid-green foliage.

FLOATING PLANTS

By cutting down the amount of light that reaches the surface of the water these plants can help to control blanket weeds and the development of algae.

AZOLLA CAROLINIANA (FAIRY MOSS, WATER FERN)

This tiny floating plant, a native to sub-tropical America, has fern-like leaves that are usually bluish-green but may be reddish.

HYDROCHARIS MORSUS-RANAE (FROGBIT)

A hardy plant, native to Europe and parts of central Asia and naturalized in some areas of North America, it resembles a miniature, white-flowered water lily. The rosettes of kidney-shaped, dark green or bronze-green leaves die down in winter, and it is not usually available for planting until late spring or early summer.

The floating water plant *Hydrocharis morsus-ranae.*

LEMNA (DUCKWEED)

All of the duckweeds should be introduced with caution – they can easily get out of hand. Found throughout the world, they are very small perennial, hardy plants. *L. polyrhiza* (syn. *Spirodela polyrhiza*, greater duckweed), has round leaves, about 6mm (¼in) across, and is a vigorous grower. *L. trisulca* (ivy-leaved duckweed, star duckweed), perhaps the prettiest of the genus, floats just below the water's surface and is an excellent water purifier.

STRATIOTES ALOIDES (WATER SOLDIER, WATER CACTUS)

Native to Europe and northwest Asia, this unusual plant has rosettes of rather spiny leaves. It bears white, cup-shaped flowers, which are sometimes tinged with pink. Although it is a useful oxygenating plant, it can spread rapidly and should be introduced with care.

MARGINAL PLANTS

The shallow water and muddy conditions around the edge of a pool are ideal for many plants that enjoy having their roots submerged in water. The plants in this section are suitable for shallow water or wet mud, and some will grow in both.

ACORUS CALAMUS 'VARIEGATUS' (SWEET FLAG)

Originally from eastern Asia but now naturalized in Europe and North America, this is a plant for shallow water. The strap-like leaves, which can reach heights of 60cm (2ft), are variegated with bright yellow. Look out for entirely green leaves and remove them, or the plant will revert to its unvariegated form.

ALISMA PLANTAGO-AQUATICA (WATER PLANTAIN)

Occurring throughout the northern hemisphere, this hardy plant will grow with up to 15cm (6in) of water above its crown. It has bright green, slightly heart-shaped leaves, borne on long stems, and the conical panicles of pinkish-white flowers are 30cm (12in) high.

BUTOMUS UMBELLATUS (FLOWERING RUSH)

This widely occurring hardy species is native to Europe, including Britain, and is naturalized in parts of North America. It has long, green leaves, and the slender stems, 90cm (3ft) or more high, bear umbels of three-petalled, rose-pink flowers in summer. Although it is really a marginal plant, *B. umbellatus* will grow in water up to 25cm (10in) deep.

CALLA PALUSTRIS (BOG ARUM, MARSH CALLA)

A native to Europe, northern Asia and North America, this hardy species should not be confused with *Zantedeschia aethiopica*, which is sometimes called the calla lily. *Calla palustris* forms mats of small, heart-shaped leaves and bears white spathes, which are sometimes followed by red berries. It is also a useful plant for disguising the edges of ponds and streams, and it will grow in up to 10cm (4in) of water. In the right conditions it may need checking.

CALTHA

This genus of marginal and bog plants contains hardy, perennial species that are grown for their attractive flowers.

C. leptosepala
This North American plant grows 15cm (6in) high and bears white, buttercup-like flowers in spring above heart-shaped, dark green leaves.

C. palustris (marsh marigold, kingcup)
This beautiful, clump-forming, marginal plant is widely distributed throughout Europe and North America. It will grow to 30cm (12in) high in water up to 7.5cm (3in) deep, and has round, dark green leaves and golden, cup-shaped flowers, which appear in spring. The variety 'Flore Plena', which is slightly more compact, bears clusters of double, bright yellow flowers, and it may produce a second flush of flowers. It is a first-class choice for both large and small water gardens.

C. polypetala
This species, which is native to eastern Europe, is larger, in both flower and leaf, than *C. palustris*. It spreads over wet ground and into shallow water, bearing bright, golden-yellow flowers. It is a vigorous plant and is not suitable for small pools or streams.

CARDAMINE PRATENSIS (CUCKOO FLOWER, LADY'S SMOCK)

This pretty, hardy plant, a native to north Europe, bears lavender flowers in early spring. It is perhaps better suited to a wild garden, for it tends to spread. The variety 'Flore Pleno' is equally lovely but does not spread as freely. They grow to 45cm (18in) high.

CAREX

The members of the sedge family are hardy, evergreen, rhizomatous perennials. Some sedges grow in water; others prefer well-drained soil.

C. elata (syn. *C. stricta*) 'Aurea' (tufted sedge)
You will sometimes find this sold as *C. elata* 'Bowles Golden' and under its common name. It thrives in a sunny position, where it will grow to 40cm (16in). The arching, golden-yellow leaves last all year round, and in summer it bears blackish-brown flower spikes. Do not let it dry out.

C. morrowii 'Variegata'

This colourful dwarf sedge grows to about 20cm (8in) and has yellow variegated foliage. It is a lovely plant to brighten a dark area.

C. pendula (pendulous sedge)

Although it can be a little coarse, this tuft-forming perennial is useful in the wild garden. It has drooping, narrow, green leaves, 45cm (18in) or more long, and pendent, greenish-brown flower spikes appear in summer. It will tolerate shade and will grow in woodland.

C. riparia (greater pond sedge)

This is a smaller sedge, growing to 60cm (2ft) or so. In the right conditions, it will quickly colonize. The variety *C. r.* 'Variegata' has narrow yellow-striped leaves and bears brown flowers in summer.

COTULA CORONOPIFOLIA (BRASS BUTTONS, GOLDEN BUTTONS)

A delightful plant from the southern hemisphere, this is also suitable for shallow water. The small, button-like yellow flowers are borne in summer, and the small, narrow, toothed leaves give off a pleasant scent when they are crushed. A hardy plant, it grows 15–30cm (6–12in) high.

HOUTTUYNIA CORDATA

A moisture-loving, hardy plant, native to the Far East, that is useful in both shallow water and at pool margins; in marshy conditions it can be invasive. The creeping, reddish stems, to 30cm (12in) long, bear small, bluish-green, heart-shaped leaves. The stems are produced from underground runners. In full sun, the leaves take on shades of red and gold. The creamy-white flowers are small. The variety 'Flore Pleno' is less invasive, and the leaves are pleasantly fragrant.

IRIS

This is a large genus, and some of the species are described in the next section, Moisture-loving Plants. The plants listed here, however, are more suitable for pool margins or even shallow water. The plants have sword-shaped leaves.

I. laevigata

This is a rhizomatous, beardless Japanese iris, which can grow to 90cm

Iris laevigata variegata is valued for both its flower and its foliage.

(3ft) high or more. It grows well in shallow water, and the flowers, which appear in early summer, are available in a range of colours. *I. l.* 'Alba', which is 45cm (18in) tall, has white flowers; *I. l.* 'Atropurpurea', also 45cm (18in) tall, has vivid blue blooms; *I. l.* 'Mottled Beauty' has white flowers, marked with blue; *I. l.* 'Murakumo', which has large, deep blue flowers with gold markings, is a free-flowering hybrid that is well worth looking out for although it is not widely available; and *I. l.* 'Variegata' has pale lavender-blue flowers enhanced by cream and green leaves.

I. pseudacorus (yellow flag)

This is a robust, beardless, rhizomatous species that is found in rivers and canals. *I. p. bastardii* has soft, creamy-yellow flowers, and *I. p.* 'Variegata' has prominent yellow stripes on the leaves in spring. The forms should not be allowed to seed.

I. × *robusta* 'Gerald Darby'

This Louisiana hybrid is a most attractive plant. In spring the sword-shaped leaves have dark purple, almost black bases, and the pretty violet-blue flowers are borne on black, branching stems 60cm (2ft) long. It is a vigorous plant and will encroach into the water from a marginal site.

I. versicolor (blue flag, wild iris)

A native to North America, the distinctive blue flowers of the rhizomatous, beardless iris are borne on stems 60cm (2ft) long. *I. v.* 'Kermesina' has reddish-purple flowers.

JUNCUS EFFUSUS F. *SPIRALIS* (CORKSCREW RUSH)

This attractive and unusual marginal plant, which is probably native to Japan, has leafless, twisted and curled stems. A hardy plant, it bears dense panicles of brownish-green flowers in summer and grows to 90cm (3ft) high.

LYSICHITON

These perennial marginal and bog plants have handsome spathes and foliage. Both species mentioned here produce large leaves after flowering, and they are too large for small pools and streams. The plants are hardy, but the young leaves can be burnt by frost.

The decorative foliage of the submerged oxygenator *Elodea canadensis* and *Mentha aquatica* require full sun.

L. americanus (yellow skunk cabbage)

The greenish-yellow spears of this North American native pierce the wet, boggy ground in early spring and form arum lily-like, bright yellow spathes. When these die back, the large, lush, green leaves, 90cm (3ft) high, appear. This is too vigorous a plant for narrow streams, and its flowers, though striking, smell unpleasant.

L. camtschatcensis

A native to Japan, this is not such a vigorous grower as *L. americanus* and is, therefore, better suited to smaller pools and streams. The pure white spathes appear before the bright green leaves, which are 75cm (30in) long.

MENTHA AQUATICA (WATER MINT)

A hardy native to north Europe, this is a vigorous and aromatic plant. The hairy, toothed leaves are almost hidden by the spires of pale lavender flowers, 23cm (9in) long, which appear in summer. Like all mints, it has a creeping rootstock and can be invasive, so it is not recommended for small streams and pools.

PONTEDERIA CORDATA (PICKEREL WEED)

In late summer this hardy native to North and South America bears spikes of attractive blue flowers, which emerge between heart-shaped, dark green leaves. It is one of the easiest of the marginal plants to grow.

RANUNCULUS LINGUA (SPEARWORT)

A handsome member of the buttercup family that is native to Europe and temperate Asia, this plant has fleshy, lance-shaped, glaucous leaves, stout stems and clusters of yellow flowers. It can reach 90cm (3ft) and is a rampant grower, which is best suited to larger pools. Look out for the variety *R. l.* 'Grandiflora', which has pinkish-green stems and larger flowers.

SAGITTARIA SAGITTIFOLIA 'FLORE PLENO' (SYN. *S. JAPONICA*) (JAPANESE ARROWHEAD)

This hardy variety is slower growing than other members of the genus. The acutely arrow-shaped leaves are upright and mid-green, and the spikes of double white flowers, 45cm (18in) tall, will grow in 7.5–15cm (3–6in) of water.

SCIRPUS LACUSTRIS SUBSP. *TABERNAEMONTANI* 'ZEBRINUS'

This striking European rush, which is suitable for shallow pool margins, has horizontally striped, brown and white spikelets. Hardy, it will grow to 1.5m (5ft) tall and will spread indefinitely.

TYPHA (REEDMACE, CAT'S TAIL)

These common marginal plants occur throughout the world and are grown for their cylindrical seedheads. They are fully hardy.

T. latifolia (great reedmace)

This species, sometimes known as common bulrush, which can achieve heights of 2.4m (8ft), is the giant of the family and is not suitable for small gardens, as it is vigorous and invasive. Spikes of beige flowers are borne above the mid-green leaves and are followed by attractive dark brown seedheads.

T. minima

This dwarf species grows to 45cm (18in) high and has rusty-brown flowers on stiff stems and graceful, narrow leaves.

T. stenophylla (syn. *T. laxmanii*)

Although it is taller – to 1.2m (4ft) – than *T. minima*, it is not as invasive.

ZANTEDESCHIA AETHIOPICA (ARUM LILY, CALLA LILY)

This native to South Africa is not a reliably hardy species, but it is undeniably beautiful. It will grow in 15–30cm (6–12in) of water as a marginal plant and has glossy, arrow-shaped leaves, 30cm (1ft) long. The pure white spathes contain golden-yellow pokers and, in the right conditions, are borne throughout the summer. The variety 'Crowborough' flowers in early summer and grows to 90cm (3ft) with a spread of 45cm (18in).

MOISTURE-LOVING PLANTS

The essential difference between the species in this group and the marginal plants described above is that while the following will thrive in moist ground most of them do not like water-logged soil.

ANEMONE RIVULARIS

A hardy perennial from eastern Asia, this summer-flowering anemone bears white, cup-shaped blooms on branching, rather stiff stems. The dark green leaves are deeply cut. It grows to about 60cm (2ft) and has a spread of about 30cm (1ft).

ASTILBE

This genus of hardy, summer-flowering perennials originated in China. The flowers are borne in tapering panicles, and there are now over a hundred garden hybrids bearing blooms of almost every colour you could wish – there is sure to be a variety to suit you. Astilbes have attractive mid-green to dark green foliage, and the brown seedheads should be left on over winter.

A. × *arendsii* 'Ceres'
A clear, light pink, late-flowering variety that can grow to 90cm (3ft).

A. × *arendsii* 'Fanal'
This is one of the best-known astilbes. It has dark crimson flowers – so dark that they are not to everyone's taste – borne early in the summer on 60cm (2ft) stems. The leaves are crimson.

A. × *arendsii* 'Ostrich Plume'
The tiny, coral-pink flowers, which appear in late summer, are borne on arching stems, 90cm (3ft) high. It looks particularly fine grown in association with *A. × thunbergii* 'Professor van der Wielen'.

A. × *arendsii* 'Venus'
Although this is an old cultivar, it is worth growing for its pretty, pale pink flowers. It has pale green, deeply cut foliage. It reaches about 90cm (3ft).

A. × *arendsii* 'White Gloria'
The stiff, erect stems, which reach about 60cm (2ft) high, carry dense spikes of white flowers in early summer. The leaves are bright green.

A. *rivularis*
Although this species is not as easily found as some of the cultivars, it is well worth looking out for. It is an elegant but robust plant, with a basal clump of deeply divided, pale green leaves, from which arise the arching, greenish-white flower stems. It spreads by means of underground runners and would be at home in a wild garden.

A. × *simplicifolia* 'Sprite'
A dwarf cultivar that grows to about 50cm (20in), so it is ideal for the front of a border and for small gardens. The feathery, shell-pink flowers appear above the finely toothed, coppery-bronze foliage.

A. taquetii

This distinctive late-flowering species bears long, erect stems of vivid magenta flowers, 90cm (3ft) high.

A. taquetii 'Superba'

This is a particularly good, robust cultivar from the species.

A. × *thunbergii* 'Professor van der Wielen'

This large plant can grow to 1.2m (4ft) high. It bears large, gracefully arching sprays of white flowers.

EUPATORIUM

This is a large genus containing hardy, half-hardy and tender shrubs, sub-shrubs and perennials, many of which are evergreen.

E. cannabinum (hemp agrimony)

This is a large, handsome plant that, in Britain at least, is generally regarded as a weed. Nevertheless, its tiny pink florets, borne on 90cm (3ft) high stems, do have a place in the wild stream garden. It has dark green, felty leaves.

E. purpureum (Joe Pye weed)

This is an imposing plant for the back of a border, and in the right conditions it can grow to 2.1m (7ft) high. In late summer and early autumn its tall stems are topped by flat heads of pinkish-purple flowers. It has dark green, pointed leaves. Despite its height, it does not need staking. There is also a dull white form.

EUPHORBIA (SPURGE, MILKWEED)

This large and widely distributed genus contains some 2,000 species of shrubs, succulents and perennials.

E. griffithii

This species, which originally came from the Himalayas, is easy to grow in heavy soil. In summer it bears dark red bracts, and the pale green leaves have red veins. The variety 'Fireglow' has orange-red bracts, and another variety worth looking out for is 'Dixter'.

E. sikkimensis

Also, as its name suggests, from the Himalayas, this species has bright red stems in spring followed by large inflorescences of pale greenish-

yellow bracts. The leaves are tinted a soft pale green. It can grow to 1.2m (4ft).

Euphorbia griffithii 'Fireglow' spreads slowly and is good for a clay soil.

FILIPENDULA (MEADOWSWEET)

This genus of hardy herbaceous perennials is found throughout Europe and Asia. They will thrive in full sun provided the soil is not allowed to dry out.

F. palmata (syn. *Spiraea digitata*)

This summer-flowering meadowsweet, which grows to about 60cm (2ft) high, carries a raspberry-red flower head and has dark green, lobed leaves. It is tolerant of shade and will form bold clumps.

F. ulmaria 'Aurea'

A lovely, leafy form of the native British meadowsweet. It has bright golden-yellow foliage in spring and in mid-summer it bears clusters of creamy-white flowers. It grows to about 30cm (12in) high.

GENTIANA (GENTIAN)

A genus containing about 400 species of hardy annuals, biennials and perennials, which are grown for their, usually, blue flowers.

G. asclepiadea (willow gentian)

This native to Europe is an excellent plant for deep, moist soil. The slender, graceful stems, up to 90cm (3ft) long and with narrow, oval leaves, carry lovely blue flowers in the axils near the tops of the stems. When it is well established it will seed itself, although the seedlings will not come true. *G. a. alba.* a white form, is a plant of which a garden cannot have too many, while 'Knightshayes' has deep blue flowers with white throats.

GUNNERA

This genus of summer-flowering perennials from South America includes some striking architectural plants that are, unfortunately, not reliably hardy. In cold areas they need winter protection in the form of compost or bracken.

G. manicata

This plant is suitable for large gardens, and it needs to be near water. It will grow to 1.8m (6ft) or more high and have a spread of 2.1m (7ft). The dark green, rounded, prickly leaves are enormous – to 1.5m (5ft) across. In early summer it bears conical spikes of light green flowers, and these are followed by orange-brown seed pods.

G. tinctoria (syn. *G. chilensis*)

This foliage plant has a height and spread of 1.5m (5ft) or more, and the large, round leaves can be 45–60cm (18–24in) across. In early summer it bears conical clusters of reddish-green flowers.

HEMEROCALLIS (DAYLILY)

Originally from Asia, there is now a wide range of cultivars, all of which are worthy of a place in the stream garden. They are generally easy to grow, long lived and trouble free, although slugs can be a problem in spring when young foliage first appears. Although each flower lasts for only a day, they are borne in succession. Most cultivars grow 60cm–1.2m (2–4ft) high. They thrive in sun or shade and are easily propagated by division in spring or autumn. Cultivars raised from seed do not come true. The following are just a few of the many named varieties now available.

H. 'Cartwheels'

This is a real eye-catcher, with huge, wide-petalled, golden-yellow flowers which open out almost flat.

H. 'Corky'

This miniature variety, which grows to 45cm (18in), has dainty, clear yellow flowers. It is lovely at the water's edge or at the front of a bed or border.

H. *fulva* 'Flore Pleno'

This is sometimes sold as 'Kwanso Flore Pleno'. It is an old and popular variety, with double, orange flowers. A vigorous grower, it will reach a height of 90cm (3ft).

H. 'Golden Chimes'

Growing to 75cm (30in), this is a graceful variety with delicate, trumpet-shaped, golden-yellow flowers, which are borne in arching sprays.

H. 'Lavender Parade'

The clear lavender flowers have greenish-yellow throats.

H. 'Lemon Balls'

This variety has lemon-yellow flowers that have a dark brown reverse to the petals.

H. 'Marion Vaughn'

The petals are a wonderfully clear yellow.

H. 'Red Precious'

The star-shaped flowers are a brilliant red.

H. 'Stafford'

This is a deservedly popular variety with mahogany-red flowers with mahogany and yellow throats.

HOSTA (PLANTAIN LILY, FUNKIA)

This genus of perennials originated in the Far East, but, as with the *Hemerocallis*, much work has been done in the development of new garden cultivars. Many of the older varieties still hold their own, however. Hostas are grown mainly for their decorative foliage, and they are excellent for ground cover. Having said that, they are generally underestimated as flowering plants – they have very attractive racemes of trumpet-shaped flowers. Slugs can be a problem. Most species prefer shade and moist, but well-drained soil. Propagate by division in the spring; seed-raised plants rarely come true to type.

H. crispula

The undulate leaves have striking white margins, and pale lilac flowers are borne early in the year. This species needs protection from the wind, which will brown the leaf edges.

H. fortunei

A group of clump-forming and vigorous hybrid perennials. They have grey-green leaves and lilac flowers. In the right conditions these plants can be very floriferous. *H. f.* 'Albopicta' has pale green leaves with creamy-yellow centres and lilac flowers. *H. f.* 'Aurea' is a lovely variety: the leaves are yellow when they first emerge but fade to green as they age.

H. 'Honeybells'

This North American hybrid, now widely available in Britain, has pale green leaves. Its main attraction is the scented, pale lilac flowers.

H. rectifolia 'Tall Boy'

This distinctive variety produces erect flower stems 1.2m (4ft) high and hung with bells of purple-pink, above fresh green, pointed foliage. It can grow to a height of 1m (3ft).

H. 'Royal Standard'

Another North American hybrid, this has fragrant flowers that are all the more welcome for appearing late in the year. The blooms are a blushing white and are borne above pale green leaves. A good subject for a container.

H. sieboldiana

The large leaves are glaucous blue, and the flowers are white with a lilac tinge. An improved, more floriferous form is *H. s.* var. *elegans*, which has large, round and deeply veined blue-grey leaves.

H. ventricosa

The broad, undulate, heart-shaped leaves, which make a handsome clump, are rich, dark and glossy green. The flowers are a darker shade of lilac than occurs in most hostas.

IRIS

This lovely, hardy genus is widely distributed in the northern hemisphere, but interestingly no species occur naturally in the southern hemisphere. Some irises require hot weather and well-drained soil, but those listed here will suit the moist, well-nourished soil conditions obtaining in a stream garden.

I. chrysographes

This free-flowering, rhizomatous, beardless Siberian iris grows about 40cm (16in) tall. The flowers, which range from reddish-purple to purple-black, are borne in late spring to early summer. The form 'Black Knight' has very dark flowers.

I. ensata (syn. I. kaempferi) (Japanese flag)

A rhizomatous, bearded, Japanese iris that will grow to 60–90cm (2–3ft). When it is grown in rich, lime-free, moist soil the stately stems bear large, sumptuous, purple or purple-red flowers.

I. sibirica (Siberian flag)

A rhizomatous, beardless iris, which grows from 50cm to 1.2m (20in to 4ft). It is a favourite plant for moist situations, although it will grow, if less well, in drier places. It is a hardy plant and will thrive for many years. The flowers can range in colour from pure white to deep purple, and they are borne above the clumps of narrow leaves. There are many named cultivars; those listed here are reliable and will grow to about 60cm (2ft). *I. s.* 'Anniversary' has ruffled white flowers; *I. s.*

'Caesar' is brilliant violet-blue; *I. s.* 'Heavenly Blue', an old cultivar, has pale sky-blue flowers; *I. s.* 'Helen Astor' is an unusual colour – dark rosy-red with white veins; *I. s.* 'Purple Cloak' has purple-blue flowers; *I. s.* 'Tropic Night' is a fine cultivar with deep blue flowers; and *I. s.* 'Wisley White' is one of the best white cultivars.

LIGULARIA

The perennials in this genus are grown for their foliage and large, daisy-like flowers. They are fully to half-hardy.

L. dentata (syn. *Senecio clivorum*)

This summer-flowering species is native to China. It should be grown in partial shade so that the large, heart-shaped leaves do not get scorched. The vivid, orange flowers are borne on stems 60cm (2ft) high. *L. d.* 'Desdemona' is a widely available cultivar that can grow to 1.2m (4ft) high. The striking, large, bronze-green leaves have red undersides. *L. d.* 'Othello' is very similar.

L. przewalskii

This clump-forming perennial has round, dark green and deeply cut leaves. The yellow flowers are borne in summer in narrow spires on black stems, 90–120cm (3–4ft) tall. It must be kept in moist soil. *L. p.* 'The Rocket' is a good form.

LUNARIA (HONESTY)

These hardy plants, native to Europe, are grown for their flowers and, just as often, for their silvery seedheads.

L. annua

This is the common biennial. It has white to deep purple flowers, borne in spring and early summer, and pointed leaves. It grows to about 75cm (30in).

L. rediviva

The perennial species bears white or lilac flowers in spring and oval, sometimes reddish, mid-green leaves.

LYSIMACHIA (LOOSESTRIFE)

These hardy summer-flowering perennials and annuals are suitable for borders as well as stream gardens.

L. clethroides
This native to China and Japan is an unusual plant for moist soil. It is vigorous and clump forming, and the stems, 60cm (2ft) high, bear spikes of white flowers in late summer.

L. ephemerum
A native of south west Europe, this has white flowers and grey foliage.

L. punctata (garden loosestrife)
This should be introduced into small gardens with caution for it can become a weed. In the wild garden its deep yellow flowers will make a striking show throughout the summer. The flower spikes, 60–75cm (24–30in) high, are borne above mid-green leaves.

LYTHRUM SALICARIA (PURPLE LOOSESTRIFE)

Widely distributed throughout northern temperate areas and in Australia, the clear pink flowers of L. salicaria are often seen growing wild along canal and river banks in late summer. It has dull green leaves and will grow to 75cm (30in). Several cultivars have been developed, and two particularly good forms are L. s. 'The Beacon' and L. s. 'Firecandle'.

MIMULUS

These moisture-loving annuals and perennials form masses of light green foliage and antirrhinum-like flowers. They are hardy and flower in summer.

M. 'Bees' Scarlet'
This hybrid, which is not widely available but is well worth looking out for, has bright red flowers.

M. cupreus 'Whitecroft Scarlet'
This is a short-lived plant, 20–30cm (8–12in) high, with freely borne, scarlet flowers.

M. luteus (monkey musk, water musk)
Native to Chile, this is a colourful waterside plant. The yellow flowers, which have reddish blotches on the petals, are borne in mid-summer on hollow stems 10–45cm (4–18in) long. When you buy this, make sure you do not inadvertently obtain M. moschatus (musk) or M. guttatus instead, as these are both rampant growers.

M. 'Red Emperor'
Sometimes sold as 'Roter Kaiser', this hybrid has brilliant crimson flowers.

M. ringens (lavender musk)
This aquatic plant, native to eastern North America, has tall, erect and much branched stems. It is unusual among aquatic plants in having lavender-blue flowers.

PELTIPHYLLUM PELTATUM (SYN. DARMERA PELTATA) (UMBRELLA PLANT)

This native to North America is a spreading perennial that will tolerate full sun or partial shade. Clusters of white or pale pink flowers are borne on white-haired stems in spring. The large, round leaves, 30cm (1ft) across, appear later. The plant will grow to 1.2m (4ft) high with a spread of 60cm (2ft). *P. p.* 'Nana', which grows to 30cm (1ft), is ideal for small gardens.

POLYGONATUM × HYBRIDUM (SOLOMON'S SEAL)

Occurring throughout Europe and north Asia, this is a hardy perennial that will tolerate a range of soil types and aspects. In late spring it bears clusters of greenish-white, pendent flowers. The arching leaves are mid-green. *P.* × *hybridum* grows 45–60cm (18–24in) high with a spread of 60cm (3ft).

PRIMULA

There are about 500 species in this genus of hardy and half-hardy perennials that are found throughout the northern hemisphere, and many of them are suitable for the stream garden. The Candelabra primulas, which have tubular, flat-faced flowers borne in whorls up the stem, are particularly useful, but the common primrose, *P. vulgaris*, should not be overlooked. All the species listed here require humus-rich soil. Many will self-seed readily, while the others may be easily divided.

P. bulleyana
A Candelabra primula with orange flowers, which appear in early summer. It will grow to 60cm (2ft) high with a spread of 30cm (1ft). The dark green leaves are toothed. An interesting feature, found also in some other species of primula, is the white 'meal' on the stems.

P. denticulata (drumstick primula)

A reliable, hardy plant that flowers in early spring. The round heads are borne on stiff, stout stems. Colours range from white and lavender to purple and red. Can be propagated by division or by seed.

P. florindae (giant cowslip)

This statuesque hardy plant has flower stems 90cm (3ft) high, rising from the toothed, mid-green leaves and bearing large heads of pendent, bell-shaped, yellow flowers throughout the summer.

P. helodoxa

Another Candelabra primula, this, too, has white 'meal' on the 90cm (3ft) stems. The bell-shaped flowers are yellow and borne in summer, and the toothed leaves are pale green.

P. japonica

This fully hardy Candelabra primula grows 30–60cm (1–2ft) high. In early summer it bears deep red, tubular flowers on stout stems above pale green, toothed, rather coarse leaves. P. j. 'Miller's Crimson' has beautifully deep crimson flowers; P. j. 'Postford White' bears white blooms. Both come true from seed.

P. pulverulenta

One of the most popular of the Candelabra primulas, this can grow to 90cm (3ft) high. The white 'meal' covering the flower stems makes it easy to identify. The whorls of magenta flowers, which have purple eyes, are borne in early summer. The mid-green leaves are toothed and lance shaped. It will thrive in sun or shade as long as the soil is moist.

P. rosea

This hardy, early-flowering species is a delight. The rose-pink flowers are borne in small clusters on short stems, 15cm (6in) high. The mid-green leaves are often flushed with bronze, and they die down completely in winter.

RHEUM PALMATUM 'ATROSANGUINEUM'

This hardy species is native to China. This variety of the clump-forming perennial, which is a member of the rhubarb family, has large, lobed leaves that are reddish-purple when young. Fluffy panicles of red flowers appear in early summer. The plant needs a lot of space – it can achieve a height and spread of 1.8m (6ft).

RODGERSIA

All members of this genus of hardy, summer-flowering perennials, native to China, are suitable for pond-side or bog-garden planting.

R. aesculifolia

An architectural plant, which will grow in sun or shade, this species has broad, bronze-tinged leaves (similar to horse chestnut leaves), which are a delightful foil for the feathery plumes of white flowers. It has a height and spread of 90cm (3ft).

R. pinnata 'Superba'

This deservedly popular variety has divided, bronze-tinged, bright green leaves and long panicles of star-shaped, bright pink flowers. It can grow to 1.2m (4ft) high.

R. tabularis (syn. Astilboides tabularis)

A handsome species, with large, circular leaves, which are attached to the stem in the centre of the leaf. The creamy-white flowers are borne on tall stems, 1.5m (5ft) above the light green leaves.

SCHIZOSTYLIS COCCINEA (KAFFIR LILY)

Although not reliably frost hardy – it is native to South Africa – this is a wonderful plant for the stream garden in warmer areas because of its early autumn flowers – bright scarlet and star shaped. The grassy foliage, 45cm (18in) long, grows in clumps, and the plants benefit from division every few years. Do this in spring. *S. c.* 'Major' is a larger, improved form; *S. c.* 'Mrs Hegarty' has pale salmon-pink flowers; *S. c.* 'Sunrise', a newish cultivar, has large, pink flowers, which appear late in the year; and *S. c.* 'Viscountess Byng' is a pink, late autumn-flowering variety.

TROLLIUS (GLOBEFLOWER)

These spring- or summer-flowering perennials, most with yellow or orange flowers, thrive near pools. Native to eastern Europe and Asia, they are hardy and will tolerate sun or shade.

T. europaeus

Pale yellow, round flowers are borne in spring above mid-green, divided leaves. The plants grow to 60cm (2ft) high. *T. e.* 'Superbus' is a superior form.

Opposite: Trollius europaeus. A good form of this attractive perennial.

T. ledebourii (syn. *T. chinensis*)
Orange, globe-shaped flowers are borne on stems 90cm (3ft) tall. The leaves are rounded and deeply divided. *T. e.* 'Golden Queen' is a fine variety.

VERATRUM

The rhizomes of these hardy herbaceous perennials are poisonous.

V. album (white false hellebore)
This species, native to Europe and north Africa, is worthy of inclusion in the garden for both its foliage and its flowers. The large, green leaves are pleated when they emerge, and the saucer-shaped, pale green flowers are borne on stems that are 1.8m (6ft) tall. It flowers in late summer or early autumn and is an eye-catching addition to any garden.

V. nigrum (black false hellebore)
A native to Siberia and south Europe, this species has dark purple flowers, which are borne from late summer. The leaves are similar to those of *V. album*, and the plants will grow to a height of 1.8m (6ft).

V. viride
This native to North America can grow to heights of 2.1m (7ft). The leaves are mid-green, and the sprays of yellow-green flowers appear in late summer.

VERONICA BECCABUNGA (BROOKLIME)

The sprawling habit of this hardy native to Europe, Asia and northern Africa makes it a suitable plant for the wild garden. It has succulent, creeping stems, smooth leaves, and bright blue, speedwell-like flowers. It grows about 30cm (1ft) high and flowers over a long period from spring to late summer.

FERNS

Ferns are ideal subjects for the stream garden, providing shades of green from spring to late autumn. Attractive in their own right, these indispensable plants provide a restful foil to the bright colours of some of the other plants and have a wonderfully 'cooling' effect. The best time for planting is autumn or spring.

ASPLENIUM SCOLOPENDRIUM (SYN. *PHYLLITIS SCOLOPENDRIUM*) (HART'S TONGUE FERN)

The glossy green, strap-shaped fronds of this hardy fern are a lovely contrast to the finely divided fronds of other ferns. The leaves are 45–75cm (18–30in) long and are a good foil to the foliage of hostas and astilbes.

BLECHNUM SPICANT (hard fern)

A hardy evergreen, 30–75cm (12–30in) high, that makes a good clump of striking, dark green fronds. It tolerates shade.

DRYOPTERIS (BUCKLER FERN)

These ferns are fully to half-hardy, but they must be grown in shade and in moist soil.

D. dilatata (syn. *D. austriaca*) (broad buckler fern)
A beautiful, graceful plant, which can reach heights of 90cm (3ft), that is native to the far north of Europe. The fronds are a lovely rusty-brown when they emerge in spring.

The hart's tongue fern, *Asplenium scolopendrium*, is a good plant for shady areas.

D. erythrosora

A native to China and Japan, this superb fern has broad fronds, rusty-brown at first but turning dark, glossy green as they age. It has a height and spread of 45–60cm (18–24in). The leaves persist until mid-winter. It is not as easy to find as some of the other ferns, but is well worth looking out for.

D. felix-mas (male fern)

Although this is common throughout temperate areas of Europe, it is worth a place in any garden – and may even self-seed. The much divided foliage is graceful but robust, and the plants will tolerate a wide range of soils. In mild areas it is evergreen. It has a height and spread of 60–120cm (2–4ft).

D. pseudomas (syn. D. borreri) (golden-scaled male fern, scaly male fern)

A robust plant that is especially beautiful in spring, when the unfurling fronds are burnished light green. The stalks are thickly covered in golden brown scales. It is a tall, elegant plant, with a height and spread of 60–90cm (2–3ft).

D. wallichiana

Similar to *D. pseudomas* in terms of colour and dimensions, this is a lovely plant, with pale brown scales all over the fronds.

MATTEUCCIA STRUTHIOPTERIS (OSTRICH FERN, OSTRICH FEATHER FERN, SHUTTLECOCK FERN)

A hardy, moisture-loving plant, which occurs throughout the northern hemisphere, this will eventually form a short stem, with a circle of pale green fronds surrounding an inner circle of shorter, dark brown fronds. When the fern is growing freely you should thin out some of the plants produced from the rhizomes so that the attractive form of the individual 'shuttlecock' is not lost. Plants grow to 1.5m (5ft) high and have a spread of 60–90cm (2–3ft).

ONOCLEA SENSIBILIS (SENSITIVE FERN)

This hardy native to North America and north Asia grows to 60cm (2ft) high. In the right conditions – that is, moist, humus-rich soil – the running rootstock can prove invasive, although it can be a useful ground-cover plant, especially among trees and shrubs. The fresh, pale green fronds are often pinkish-brown in spring. In autumn, the fronds become an attractive yellowish-brown.

OSMUNDA

A genus of large, deciduous, hardy ferns. Remove all fading fronds regularly.

O. cinnamomea (cinnamon fern)
This graceful North American species will grow to 90–120cm (3–4ft) high. At first the fronds are covered with a woolly, brown coating, but they eventually become a fresh green.

O. claytoniana (interrupted fern)
The common name of this native to North America is apt, for the fronds appear to be incomplete: there are brown, fertile pinnae halfway way up the fronds so that the pale green, fertile fronds do not seem to grow all the way to the top. The plants will grow to about 60cm (2ft) high.

O. regalis (royal fern)
A native to Europe, this elegant, bright green fern will thrive in wet, boggy ground. The fronds are tinted brownish-pink at first but gradually turn green. Mature plants bear rusty-brown tassels of flower spikes. Plants can grow to 1.8m (6ft) high, although 1.2m (4ft) is more usual.

POLYSTICHUM SETIFERUM (SOFT SHIELD FERN)

A native to Europe, this hardy fern can be seen growing wild in woods and hedgerows. The plants are about 60cm (2ft) high, and the plumy, much divided, mid-green fronds are oval or lance shaped.

BULBS

It is possible to find bulbs that will provide colour throughout the year. They are indispensable in the garden, having an almost limitless range of size, leaf form and flower colour.

CARDIOCRINUM GIGANTEUM (GIANT LILY)

This imposing lily from the Himalayas is not reliably frost hardy. It bears spikes of fragrant, cream flowers, 15cm (6in) long, in summer. The flowers have purple-red streaks inside. They are followed by brown seed pods. The shiny, dark green leaves are large at the base of the plant and become smaller towards the top of the tall stems. It can grow to 2.5m (8ft).

CROCOSMIA (MONTBRETIA)

This genus of hardy corms is grown for its brightly coloured flowers, which appear in late summer. The leaves are long and sword shaped. 'Carmine Brilliant' is a good late-flowering variety with strawberry-red flowers, and 'Star of the East' has large yellow flowers, with the outer segments flushed with red. 'Citronella' which is a clear pale yellow and 'Solfaterre' – apricot-yellow with bronze foliage – are also worthy plants.

C. paniculata (syn. Curtonus paniculatus)
A bold plant to 1.5m (5ft) high that has long-tubed, orange flowers on branched stems and attractive seed pods.

FRITILLARIA MELEAGRIS (SNAKE'S HEAD FRITILLARY)

Native to northern Europe, including Britain, this hardy plant thrives in wet meadows and limy soil, where it will self-seed. The lantern-shaped flowers, which appear in late spring, are borne on graceful stems and are pale to deep pinkish-purple, sometimes chequered in white.

LEUCOJUM (SNOWFLAKE)

This genus includes autumn- and spring-flowering species, which are grown for their bell-shaped pink or white flowers. Propagate by division in spring or early autumn, or by seed in autumn. They are generally free of pests and diseases.

L. aestivum (summer snowflake)
Occurring throughout northern and central Europe, this hardy species produces robust clumps of shining, dark green, strap-shaped leaves, which are a perfect foil for the 45cm (18in) tall stems. Each stem has three or more pendent, snowdrop-like flowers with distinctive green spots. They thrive in swampy places and in ditches. The flowers appear in late spring. Look out for the variety 'Gravetye Giant', which is larger and more erect.

L. vernum (spring snowflake)
Although the flowers are similar to those of *L. aestivum*, this is a shorter plant – 30cm (12in) high – with broad green leaves. It is hardy and flowers in early spring. L. vernum does best in moist conditions and will tolerate shade.

NARCISSUS

This large genus is grown for its ornamental flowers. They prefer sun or light shade, and most cultivars increase naturally by offsets. They are hardy and there are hundreds of varieties and dozens of species to choose from.

N. cyclamineus

This delightful little narcissus from Spain and Portugal is only 15cm (6in) tall. It flowers in late winter to early spring, bearing slender, golden flowers with narrow petals and long trumpets. It thrives in damp mountain pastures, often near shady streams and rivers.

GRASSES AND SEDGES

Grasses have become more popular in gardens in recent years, and they are often used as a foil to other, more solid-looking plants. However, many grasses can be used to good effect on their own. The *Carex* species have already been discussed under Marginal Plants (see pp. 89–90).

ARUNDO DONAX (GIANT REED)

Native to southern Europe, this stately plant can grow to 2.4m (8ft) high. It grows equally well in moist and dry soil. The blue-grey leaves are broad, and flop on alternate sides of the thick, bamboo-like stems.

CORTADERIA SELLOANA (PAMPAS GRASS)

This hardy, clump-forming plant, a native to South America, may be too bold for some gardens – it is certainly not everyone's favourite plant, although in the right setting it can look dramatic, reaching 2.4m (8ft) high. *C. s.* 'Pumila' is smaller, growing to 1.5m (5ft) high, and with erect flower stems.

DESCHAMPSIA CAESPITOSA (TUFTED HAIR GRASS)

This fully hardy grass is found throughout the southern and northern hemispheres. Stems of purple flowers arise from dense tussocks of grassy, arching leaves. Dainty panicles of pale brown spikelets appear in summer and last until winter. In autumn the leaves turn a pleasant copper colour. In a damp site plants will grow to 90cm (3ft) high.

GLYCERIA MAXIMA 'VARIEGATA' (SYN. *G. AQUATICA* 'VARIEGATA')

This European plant can be invasive. The arching leaves are striped with creamy-yellow and form a mass from which the panicles are borne. It can grow to 80cm (30in) high and has an indefinite spread.

HAKONECHLOA MACRA 'AUREOLA'

Native to Japan, this is a slow-growing plant. It will appreciate a humus-rich, moisture-retentive soil. It forms a dense carpet of purple stemmed and green-striped yellow leaves, which turn reddish brown as they age. Panicles of reddish-brown flower spikes may be borne in early autumn. It grows to 40cm (16in) high.

MISCANTHUS SINENSIS (SYN. *M. JAPONICUS, EULALIA JAPONICA*)

This is a strongly growing, hardy species from China and Japan, which has narrow blue-green leaves, each with a white mid-rib. *M. s.* 'Gracillimus' has narrow-leaved, grassy foliage, which often turns bronze in autumn. Grow it as a specimen plant on a grassy bank; it will reach 1.2m (4ft) high with a spread of 45cm (18in). *M. s.* 'Silver Feather' is a first-class, autumn-flowering grass that will grow to 1.8m (6ft) high. The erect, graceful stems bear terminal, pinkish-fawn flowers. *M. s.* 'Zebrinus' (tiger grass) has leaves with yellowish-white, transverse markings and may carry hairy white spikelets. It grows to 1.2m (4ft) high and is a desirable background plant.

MOLINIA ALTISSIMA (SYN. *M. CAERULEA* SUBSP. *ARUNDINACEA*) (PURPLE MOOR GRASS)

Native to Europe, this hardy plant has slender stems of purple sprays, but it comes into its own in autumn, when the leaves turn gold. It grows to 2.4m (8ft). The variety 'Variegata' has yellow-striped, mid-green leaves and grows to 60cm (2ft).

SPARTINA PECTINATA 'AUREO MARGINATA' (SYN. *S. P.* 'AUREO-VARIEGATA')

This North American grass can be invasive, so give it plenty of space. It will reach 1.8m (6ft) high, and the narrow foliage is striped with yellow. Greenish flowers are borne in spikes. It is a good subject for a wild garden.

STIPA GIGANTEA (GOLDEN OATS)

This hardy, evergreen species comes from Spain. It is a superb plant, most attractive when in flower and shimmering in the sunlight. The dense mass of narrow leaves and the elegant, silvery spikelets arch gracefully. It can grow to 2.4m (8ft) with a spread of 90cm (3ft). Plant it where it can be viewed against the light.

TREES

The trees described here will tolerate damp conditions. Before you plant a tree, think carefully about its ultimate height and spread.

ALNUS (ALDER)

All the species in this genus will thrive in moist situations, and the flowers, in the form of catkins, are borne in late winter and early spring.

A. cordata (Italian alder)
Native to Italy, this is a moderately fast-growing, conical species with heart-shaped, glossy, dark green leaves. It is hardy and can reach a height of 20m (66ft).

A. glutinosa (black alder, common alder)
This tree occurs throughout Europe, Asia and North America. Although it is not in the front rank of decorative trees, it can be an asset to the stream garden and has attractive yellow catkins in spring. It can reach 25m (80ft). The variety *A. g.* 'Pyramidalis', which forms a narrow, conical tree, is better suited to the smaller garden.

A. incana (grey alder)
This hardy tree, native to Europe and North America, is ideal for cold, wet sites and poor soils. The oval, dark green leaves have grey undersides, which are evident in the wind. Yellow-brown catkins are carried in late winter and early spring. It grows to about 15m (50ft), although it can be grown as a shrub. The form *A. i.* 'Laciniata' has dissected leaves.

A. rubra
This hardy tree, from western North America, is one of the gems of the genus. It is a medium sized tree, with large leaves and a graceful habit. In spring it is festooned with red catkins.

AMELANCHIER (JUNEBERRY, SERVICEBERRY, SHADBUSH)

These deciduous, spring-flowering trees and shrubs are grown for their profuse flowers and the wonderful autumn colours of the foliage. They are easily grown and fully hardy.

A. laevis

This North American tree has a lovely display of white flowers, which are followed by rounded, fleshy, red fruits. The young, oval leaves are bronze, then turn green in summer before changing to shades of red and orange later in the year. It will reach about 15m (50ft) but can also be grown as a shrub.

A. lamarckii

This is more of a shrub than a tree, although it will reach a height of 6m (approximately 20ft). The leaves are silky-bronze in spring, and white flowers are borne in lax bunches. In autumn the leaves turn a rich orange-red and purple berries appear.

BETULA (BIRCH)

A genus of trees grown mostly for their bark and autumn colours; all are fully hardy.

B. nigra (river birch)

A North American species, this is one of the best trees for damp ground. It is fast growing and soon produces its shaggy, brownish-black bark. It grows up to 6m (20ft) high. It is not widely planted in Britain, where it deserves to be better known.

B. pubescens (common white birch)

If you have very damp ground plant this in preference to *B. pendula* (common silver birch). *B. pubescens* does not have such a weeping habit, but its white bark is always attractive. It grows to a height of 6–9m (20–30ft).

METASEQUOIA GLYPTOSTROBOIDES (DAWN REDWOOD)

This is a Chinese species that is most at home in moist soils, although it will tolerate dry ground. It is a lovely, upright, deciduous conifer, growing to 15m (50ft) or more. The bluish-green leaves turn yellow, pink and red in autumn. The shaggy brown bark is attractive in winter. A particularly narrow, conical form called 'National' is worth seeking for the smaller garden.

NYSSA SYLVATICA (BLACK GUM, TUPELO)

The wonderful mid-green, ovate leaves of this native to the east of North America turn scarlet and orange before they fall. A hardy tree, it grows to 15m (50ft) or more.

Nyssa sylvatica, a native of North America, is tolerant of moist, acid soils.

SALIX (WILLOW)

This is a very large genus of deciduous trees and shrubs, grown for their catkins, habit, foliage and, in some cases, for their winter colour. See also the recommended Shrubs (pp. 120–21).

S. alba (white willow)

This native to Europe and western Asia is hardy and large – to 15m (50ft) high. It is a fast-growing and elegant tree, with silvery-grey leaves and lovely, yellowish-green catkins. If pruned hard it can be grown as a shrub, which will reach 1.5–1.8m (5–6ft). *S. a.* 'Britzensis' (syn. *S. a.* 'Chermesina') has green leaves and bright orange-red young shoots. *S. a.* var. *vitellina* (golden willow), which can also be grown as a shrub, has pendulous, yellow shoots.

S. daphnoides (violet willow)

Native to northern Europe and central Asia, this fast-growing, spreading tree will, if hard pruned in spring, enhance the stream garden with long, purple-violet stems, each overlaid by a white bloom. The glossy, dark green leaves are lance shaped, and the catkins are silver. It is hardy and will grow to 15m (50ft) or more.

S. exigua (coyote willow)

This beautiful small tree or large shrub is native to western North America and Mexico. A hardy tree, it has long, slender branches adorned with narrow, silky-grey leaves and catkins in spring. It is a good alternative to *Pyrus salicifolia* 'Pendula'.

TAXODIUM DISTICHUM (SWAMP CYPRESS, BALD CYPRESS)

This broadly conical conifer is the dominant tree of the Florida Everglades, and it is suitable for very wet sites because it has specially adapted 'breathing' roots. The fresh green leaves turn rich brown in late autumn. It is hardy and grows up to 20m (66ft) high. *T. d. nutans* (syn. *T. ascendens nutans*) is a slow-growing, architectural tree of narrow, columnar shape. Its smaller size makes it better suited to small gardens than the type species.

SHRUBS

A group of carefully selected shrubs will not only give the stream garden colour and interest throughout the year, including the winter months when other plants have died back, but, as a bonus, will help to consolidate the stream banks.

CLETHRA ALNIFOLIA (SWEET PEPPER BUSH)

This hardy, bushy shrub, which has a height and spread of 2.4m (8ft), is native to eastern North America. It has sweetly scented, white flowers, which are borne in late summer, and delightful yellow and bronze foliage in the autumn. It is an ideal plant for wet ground. The form *C. a.* 'Paniculata' has larger flowers and narrow leaves, and *C. a.* 'Rosea' has pink flowers with glossy leaves and buds.

CORNUS (DOGWOOD)

The trees and shrubs in this genus are grown for their flowers, foliage or, especially, their brightly coloured winter stems.

C. alba (red barked dogwood)

Native to the area from Siberia to Manchuria, this robust, spreading bush – the height and spread are 3m (10ft) – is tolerant of both wet and dry conditions. The leaves colour well in the autumn, when there is also a good display of white-tinged, blue fruits. Hard pruning in late

Opposite: The dogwood, *Cornus alba* 'Siberica', should be regularly pruned to promote young, vivid red growths.

spring will encourage the production of more, brighter red stems in winter. *C. a.* 'Sibirica' is less robust but has vivid red stems.

C. stolonifera 'Flaviramea'

This is a vigorous plant, native to North America. It grows to about 1.8m (6ft) high, and has bright greenish-yellow shoots in winter.

LONICERA × *PURPUSII*

This hardy hybrid bears fragrant, creamy-white flowers in winter and early spring. It has a height and spread of 1.5m (5ft).

PHOTINA VILLOSA

This hardy shrub is native to Japan, Korea and China. A moist, but not too wet soil will suit this upright shrub best. It has a height and spread of 1.5m (5ft) and bears white, hawthorn-like flowers in late spring. These are followed by red berries, but its main attraction is the brilliant autumn colour.

RUBUS THIBETANUS

This bramble is native to western China. It has glossy dark green foliage but is chiefly grown for its white-bloomed, young shoots, which are borne in winter. Small, pink flowers appear in late summer and are followed by black fruit. It grows to about 2.4m (8ft).

SALIX (WILLOW)

Some of the trees in this genus have already been mentioned (see pp. 117–18).

S. elaeagnos (hoary willow)

This hardy, southern European shrub is upright and dense, with a height and spread of 3m (10ft). It has yellow catkins and dark green leaves with white undersides, which turn yellow in autumn.

S. hastata 'Wehrhahnii'

This hardy shrub, which is native to Switzerland, has deep purple stems and silvery-grey catkins, which are borne before the bright green foliage appears. The stems later turn yellow. It is a small, slow-growing shrub, suitable for small gardens.

S. irrorata
Another species from North America, this fully hardy shrub, which grows to 3m (10ft) high, has catkins with red, then yellow anthers and purple young shoots, which are covered with a striking white bloom.

S. 'Melanostachys' (syn. *S. gracilistyla* 'Melanostachys') (black willow)
This unusual, fully hardy large shrub or small tree bears almost black catkins with red anthers in early spring. Later, lance-shaped, bright green leaves appear.

S. repens (creeping willow)
This low-growing shrub, native to Europe and Asia, bears silky, grey catkins on naked stems in spring. The grey-green, narrowly oval leaves appear later.

VIBURNUM

This genus of trees and shrubs is grown for its foliage, autumn colour and flowers. It occurs throughout temperate regions from North America to Japan.

V. × bodnantense
This is one of the best of the winter-flowering shrubs, bearing white-flushed, rose-pink flowers in clusters in winter. It has a height and spread of 2.4m (8ft). It is hardy, although flowers can be nipped by frost. New flowers follow quickly. The cultivar 'Deben' is similar but bears flowers from late autumn to early spring.

V. opulus (guelder rose)
This is a justly popular plant. It has a height and spread of about 4m (12ft); it has flowers, fruit and autumn colour; and it is hardy and will thrive in damp conditions. The white flowers are like those of the lace-cap hydrangea; the fruit are like glistening bunches of redcurrants; and the autumn colour is provided by the maple-like, pinkish leaves. *V. o.* 'Compactum' has deep green leaves, red in autumn, and a more compact habit; *V. o.* 'Xanthocarpum' has yellow fruits and mid-green leaves that become yellow in autumn.

Appendix:
The Stream Garden Year

No garden is static – that is part of their enduring appeal – and here we provide a brief year-round maintenance programme. Use this as a checklist for the planting and care of your stream garden.

SPRING

PLANTING

Plant bog and waterside plants, digging the area well and incorporating humus. If there is still a risk of frost, make sure that any recently planted subjects are still firm in the soil.

MAINTENANCE

Thin out hostas, Siberian flags (*Iris sibirica*) and primulas. Protect hostas with slug pellets or spray; alternatively, apply a liberal coating of ashes, gritty sand or woodchips. Remove any dead or dying foliage that you missed in autumn, taking especial care with marginal plants, removing one leaf at a time, so that you do not damage them or rip them out of the soft mud completely.

POOL AND STREAM CARE

Rake off any blanket weed (an alga that grows in long, greenish-brown tresses that feel rough to the touch). Blanket weed often occurs early in the year, before the water plants have had a chance to put on vigorous growth. If blanket weed or other algae are persistent, you can buy an algicide to control the problem, although it is usually possible to remove it by simply raking it off until your other plants are strong enough to restore the proper balance in the pool.

Remove excess oxygenators from the pool early in the year, but be careful not to remove so much that tadpoles and other creatures do not have hiding places.

Check that sudden rain does not bring debris and rubbish down the watercourse, causing blockages, especially around the dams.

SUMMER

PLANTING

Now that water temperatures will have risen, introduce newly bought water plants to your pool. This will allow plants to become established before the onset of winter. In early summer new water lilies and oxygenators can be planted, as described in the Plant Directory.

MAINTENANCE

Thin out water lilies and, if necessary, divide them so that they can become established before the winter. Water lilies show when they require attention by pushing the congested foliage above the water's surface. If you have to remove containers from the deepest part of the pool you will need a pair of waders or, if the weather is very warm, swim wear. If the lilies are planted in the base of the pool you will need to cut out the growing points and replant each piece. You need about 15cm (6in) of tuber with a good, strong vigorous shoot. The tubers of some lilies grow horizontally; others have vertically growing tubers. Feed water lilies with a granular, slow-release fertilizer.

On the whole water plants have few problems. Insecticides are not to be recommended, although if plants in and around the pool suffer from aphids you can usually dislodge them with a strong spray of water. Failing that, submerge the foliage for 24 hours, holding it down with stones.

Deadheading spent flowers is worth doing to prolong the flowering period. Exceptions might be astilbes – their brown seedheads should be left on as they are an attractive feature in autumn and winter. You can also leave the large seed pods of *Cardiocrinum giganteum* and *Lysimachia ephemerum*.

POOL AND STREAM CARE

Keep blanket weed under control, raking it from the water surface if necessary. If the weather is dry and hot, evaporation, especially from shallow pools, may be considerable and you will almost certainly need to top them up.

AUTUMN

PLANTING

This is the best time of year to plant shrubs and trees, while the soil is still warm.

MAINTENANCE

Divide and replant established plants in damp areas but take care not to trample and consolidate the soil – standing on a plank helps.

POOL AND STREAM CARE

Now is the time to remove all dead and dying growth from the water. As the leaves fall from the trees, cover small pools with nets because as the leaves decompose they give off gases that are harmful to fish. Decomposing organic matter will encourage the growth of algae, so it is important to remove all dead leaves and flowers.

Take the pump from the pool and have it cleaned and ready for the following year.

WINTER

PLANTING

The coldest months of the year are a time for planning rather than planting, for browsing through catalogues and ordering plants for spring, although, if the ground is not frozen, it is possible to plant shrubs and trees at this time.

MAINTENANCE

In general there is little to do in the garden, although an early application of slug pellets around hostas may be necessary if the weather is mild. This is also a good time to apply a general mulch of mushroom compost or leaf mould, especially around those plants in the stream garden that may be exposed to the full summer sun.

POOL AND STREAM CARE

If you keep fish make sure that part of the pool is always free of ice, especially if the water is shallow. You could use a heater, but it is cheaper and just as effective to float a ball in the water.

While there is little to do, you may want to consider whether you need or would like to install a second pool, extend the stream or add a feature such as a dam or stepping-stones. Make your plans now.

Index